Retire Worry Free: Essays on Risk and Money Management

Publisher's Cataloging-in-Publication data

Nagy, Andras M.
Retire worry free : essays on risk and money management / Andras Nagy.
p. cm.
Includes bibliographical references.
ISBN 13 978-0-9753093-1-5

1. Finance, personal. 2. Retirement--Planning. 3. Investments. 4. Portfolio management. 5. Foreign exchange market. I. Title.

HG179 .N33 .R48 2006
332.0242--dc22   2006927347

All Rights Reserved © 2005 by Andras Nagy

No part of this book may be reproduced or transmitted in any form or by any means, graphic, electronic, or mechanical, including photocopying, recording, taping or by any information storage or retrieval system, without the permission in writing from the publisher.

Other Titles by Andras Nagy

Commodity Trading 101 - ISBN 978-0-9753-0930-8

Retire Worry Free: Essays on Risk and Money Management

By Andras M. Nagy

ISBN Number 978-0-9753093-1-5
LCCN Number 2006927347

Dedication

To my daughter Dora

Table of Contents

Other Titles by Andras Nagy...2
Retire Worry Free: Essays on Risk and Money Management..................................3
   By Andras M. Nagy 3
Dedication iv
Table of Contents..v
About The Author vi
Preface...vii
Introduction 10
   Background 10
Risks in Life... 11
Position Trading and Risk Management 22
Probability of Ruin 34
Asset Allocation... 50
Speculation 63
Modern Portfolio Theory.. 74
Psychology.. 77
Five Common Pitfalls 83
Position Trading 85
Position Trading and the True Range 104
Mathematical Expectation... 112
Daily Volatility 117
Position Trading Rules 124
The Futures Markets... 127
History of Futures Trading... 129
Order Entry 101 150
Charting and Indicators 154
Types of Indicators 156
Seasonal Trends and Geopolitics 101 165
Psychology.. 168
IRA Accounts for Futures 174
Gold... 175
Brokers.. 183
Trading for a Living – Should I Tell the Boss 186
Spread Trading.. 188
Volume and Open Interest 201
Why Speculators Fail?... 204
My 'super special' secrets... 210
Foreign Exchange Speculating 212
Other Useful Books to Read 222
Glossary 224
Index.. 231

About The Author

Andras Nagy has been in the investment and financial engineering field since 1986. He became a stockbroker despite a job offer from Microsoft. This is an example that demonstrates his lack of hunger for wealth and his streak of independence. This move had puzzled many including him later.

Andras had spent the last 20 years working as a futures broker with Refco, a software designer and contract engineer for various investment and trading firms.

In the late 80's after getting a grubstake together he purchased a seat at the MidAm Futures and later he also became a member at the Chicago Board of Trade. He traded options on futures and Futures Spreads.

Andras saw that trading is moving more upstairs and becoming more electronic so he abandoned his floor trading and first traded from the CBOT cafeteria then later he moved off the floor altogether. After various computer-consulting assignments he found his true love, trading again, this time in New York City. He moved there with the notion of trading futures in New York but events turned him to the stock market.

He had met Robert Kanter President of Electronic Trading Group (ETG), he personally persuaded Andras to trade stocks instead of futures. Decimalization of course put many listed traders out of business. This was no different with Andras. He had to adjust and move on.

After New York he spent years of Computer software contracting and trading his retirement account.

Andras is also interested in Poker, game theory and occasionally visiting Las Vegas. He lives in California and he mentors and consults with people who wish to transform their lives. You can ask him questions via his web site.

Editor

Preface

"There is the plain fool who does the wrong thing at all times everywhere, but there is the Wall Street fool, who thinks he must trade all the time."

Jesse Livermore

Buying and selling stocks and derivatives have increased enormously over the last decade.

An occupation, earlier restricted to a few well-situated capital owners, has now become almost a national movement. Almost half of adult Americans own stock directly or indirectly. Their numbers have increased sixty percent in the past fifteen years. A growing portion of the public depends more on Private Retirement Plans than on Social Security for their retirement income.

The stock market is a popular subject of discussion. Media has been flashing reports on people who have gained huge amounts in the markets. Equal coverage has been done on how much capital was lost in the latest decline. These reports gives hindsight descriptions of how one can make millions.

How one can make big money is the question here. During the last quarter of 1999 and first quarter of 2000, when stock market indices in the Western world soared high, everyone wondered; "buying what stock would be most profitable"? Since March 2000, during the decline, the focus has fairly changed to "how one should avoid getting ruined".

Narrowing it down to one simple question: "why do some people succeed in the markets, while others go bankrupt"?

Some possible clues can be found when reviewing the psychological research within the behavioral finance. Let us consider an example: investors adjust slowly and as a possible effect, they do not see when the bull-market turns into a bear-market. This leads them to hold their positions longer then expected. Why does this happen? We will discuss this in the coming sections and the implications in details in the chapters to follow.

Getting back to the psychological research within the behavioral finance, it has been noticed that when we as humans make decisions under uncertainty, our choices are influenced by the situation rather than the absolute value of the result. When we perceive the situation as a loosing scenario, we tend to be risk seeking. Consequently, if a scenario is perceived as positive we will become risk-averse. This explains why investors take greater risks during the big decline than they otherwise would judge as reasonable.

Altogether, these human foibles make investing or trading in the stock markets a difficult task. We will discuss more of these aspects in this book.

So how could one possibly become a successful market player? This book is a key to this question; lets look at a root solution - One of the recipes of success is to control one's risk and utilize proper "Money Management". When we discuss Money Management here, it is not "risk control" per se, "diversification" or "how one makes trading decisions" as, stated most of the times.

Risk control and maximization of profits is rather a result of implementing money management strategies. It is considered that money management or position sizing answers the question: "How much?" or "How many?" In the meaning of "how much of available capital is to be put at risk?" or "how many contracts or shares are to be bought?"

In this book the following definition of Money Management will be used: Money management determines how much of available capital is to be allocated in a specific market position, that is, the number of shares bought or percentage of total capital spent.

The science of risk-efficient portfolios is associated with a couple of guys (a couple of Nobel laureates, actually) named Harry Markowitz and Bill Sharpe. It is their work that Modern Portfolio Theory based on. This is the theme of this book along with common sense ideas and advice to the average person who wish to retire safely and without dark clouds on the fiscal horizon.

Introduction

Background

"God grant me the Serenity to accept the things I cannot change, Courage to change things I can, and Wisdom to know the difference"

Reinhold Niebuhr

In the new brave world of Globalization and economic dislocation many people in the world find themselves as if the proverbial rug was pulled out from under them.

This book focuses on the average person and his or hers chances of surviving and prospering until retirement - it does not offer *secrets* on getting rich or 'making a killing' in the markets rather it examines the path of a well-balanced life and fiscal outlook heading towards retirement.

Due to the debate on the state of Social Security and the disappearing private pensions offered by Corporations; hopefully it has become clear to most people that one cannot rely on anyone for secure retirement except one's careful savings and managing one's own money. Some people retire due to successful real estate investing.
In this book we shall focus on Stock, Currency and Commodity speculating. It is the author's firm belief that most speculators fail not because there is a giant conspiracy on Wall Street rather than the gross misconception and ill education on Risk and Portfolio Management.

Terminology used in the book "position trading' is loosely synonymous with trend-following. The unit calculation for Position Trading is based on the Percentage Volatility Model (PVM)

Risks in Life

I do not fear tomorrow, for I have seen yesterday and I love today

William Allen White

What is Risk? Risk is the chance of not having enough money when you need it, to buy something important. Risk is going against the current, taking the hard way against high odds is taking risk.

In a world of constant change, taking risks is considered to be accepting the flow of change and aligning ourselves with it. It does seem to be a reckless endangerment, but for those who understand reality, risk is considered to be actually the safest way to cope with the changing uncertain world.

To take a risk is indeed to plunge into circumstances we cannot absolutely control. But the fact is that the only circumstances in this life that we can absolutely control are so relatively few and so utterly trivial as hardly to be worth the effort. Besides, the absence of absolute control, which is impossible in any case, does not entail the absence of any control, or even significant control.

To be more specific, the sort of risks that put one in a position to control one's lot in a world of incessant change are the risks that attempt to add something of value to that world. To create value, to focus one's efforts on increasing the fund of that which is worthwhile, involves a sort of risk. And yet, paradoxically, it provides with the greatest control over a changing world and maximizes the chances to achieve a truly meaningful personal satisfaction.

The main difference between an amateur and a professional trader is that the latter always tries to understand and control portfolio risks. Before entering into any trade, good traders first think about how much risk to take and how much risk exposure comes with a particular trade selection. Only then do they allow themselves to think about how much profit they stand to make.

Prudent investors always cut down their position and exposure if they determine that a portfolio carries too much risk. They calculate this all-important estimation by employing Risk Management, that set of methods and procedures taken to estimate, quantify, and control risk for the purpose of achieving optimal investment results.

Risk management is the difference between success and failure in trading. Trading correctly is 90% money and portfolio management, a fact that most people want to avoid or don't understand.

Capitalism rewards those with the brains, guts and determination to find opportunity where others have overlooked; to press on and succeed where others have fallen short and failed. The right decisions lead to wealth and success; the wrong ones lead to bankruptcy and a redistribution of resources from weak hands to strong as capitalism rolls on.

It has been said that the amount of risk we take in life is in direct proportion to how much we want to achieve. If one wants to live boldly, then he must make bold moves. If the goals are meager and few, they can be reached easily and with less risk of failure, but with greater risk of dissatisfaction once achieved.

Some people are kiodiophobic (risk averse) while others are kiodiotropic (risk seeking). The phobes are hesitant to pull the trigger, keep their bets small and have uneventful performance. The tropes pull on any excuse, bet large and take thrilling roller coaster rides.

There are two kinds of risk, blind risk and calculated risk. Blind risk is the calling card of laziness, the irrational hope, the cold twist of fate. It is the pointless gamble, the emotional decision. The man who embraces blind risk demonstrates all the wisdom and intelligence of a drunk trying to speed through heavy traffic. Calculated risk has proven to built fortunes, nations and empires. Calculated risk and bold vision go hand in hand. Using mind, watching the possibilities, working things out logically, and then moving forward in strength and confidence, managing risk and dealing with it responsibly is what required in a successful trader.

The trick is to come to terms with one's own tendencies and find a system that honors their psychological needs and also shows profit.

For gamblers from blackjack to horse racing as well as all traders, making serious money demands they get serious. As a result, they take a completely different approach towards betting from people who enter these endeavors for the action, the excitement and, of course, the dream of winning big.

Nearly every profitable investor keeps continuous and detailed records of their trading decisions, thoughts and observations. Recording in written form forces them to function in a disciplined manner. Details on paper structure the decision making process. Anxiety, greed and fear are replaced with confidence and determination. A constant review of the decision-making process that goes into each trade is not enjoyable. But, the process of self-examination is crucial to successful trading. Keeping a journal of decision-making that records when, where, why and how much to bet on each trade or wager is a good control strategy. The idea is to reach a comfort zone, stay within that zone and to quit whenever tempted to leave it. Keeping records is a part of managing money, and if one is not disciplined in money management, he is going to lose his entire bankroll.

So controlling risk is crucial because losses determine that something is wrong. If a person doesn't know how to determine when he is wrong, then he is headed for disaster.

Developing and maintaining a record-keeping system:

- Develop and maintain a record-keeping system that works for you.

- Critique the performance in writing each day.

- Write down the personality characteristics or take a personality test.

- Write those parts of the personality that make you a successful trader, and those parts you must constantly guard against.

- Write down the trading rules and educate one as much as possible about them.

More risk controlling tips: to become even-tempered about money takes practice, one must detach emotions and ego from what he is doing. Being calm, cool and collected and not getting excited about profits will help you in preventing losses. If one cannot control greed, fear and hope then trading might not be for him.

Performance Benchmark, Beta, Correlation, Volatility and Return/Risk Ratio

If an investor bought a stock at $100 and sold it six months later at $116, then he would realize a profit of $16. His annualized return would be 32%. No doubt, this is a good investment result. Is this a better or worse investment compared with others? Without systematic analysis, we cannot tell: to properly evaluate investment performance, we need to consider the return, the risks involved, and how the outcome compares with other possible investments. In order to quantify risks and measure risk-adjusted performance, following concepts are applied:

Correlation

If the index moves up, percent of the time the stock also moves up. Please refer to the 'Portfolio Diversification' section of this book.

Beta

This serves as the measure of a portfolio's risk relative to the market; if the index moves 1 percent, then the stock moves Beta percent. In Position Trading, the beta of one currency rate is often computed with respect to another currency rate.

Volatility

For trading applications, daily volatility is a very useful measure of risk: percent of the time, stock price moves up or down percent in a day. It is important to know the difference between this daily volatility and the annualized volatility, which is used in stock option and derivatives valuation.

Return/Risk Ratio

The Return/Risk Ratio is defined as R/v, the higher the ratio the better the performance. If we plot the return against risk for many different kinds of investments, we get a chart like that presented in Figure below:

Zero-Risk Investment might be likened to a bank account that earns risk-free interest. At the other extreme, some individual stocks are extremely risky, leading to a great variation in the range of potential return or loss. In examining many different kinds of investments over long-term periods (say ten years), a graphic representation would appear like a cloud with a rather clear upper boundary - the so-called "Efficient Market Frontier." If an investment lies on the efficient frontier, it is considered "optimal" or "advantageous.

Investing/Speculating is a "zero-sum" game. On average, passively buying currency contracts and holding them does not generate returns. A successful trader makes positive returns by trading skillfully and consistently.

Sharp Ratio

The Sharp Ratio is a measure of a portfolio's excess return relative to the total variability of the portfolio. It is named after William Sharp, Nobel Laureate, and inventor of the capital asset pricing model. Let the annualized return of the portfolio be R, the risk free interest rate r, and the annualized volatility v, then the Sharp Ratio is (R-r)/v. It is equally applicable to equity, fixed-income, commodity traders and fund managers.

VAR (Value At Risk)

Most leading investment and trading houses use VAR as one of their main risk measures in routine risk-management operations. VAR is an absolute risk measure for the portfolio, in units of dollars per day. In a single trading day, there is a 95% probability that the portfolio will not lose more than VAR. For example, if the VAR value is $800, then one can assume that it is 95% certain that the portfolio will not lose more than $800 in one day.

Hedging

Hedging means the specific actions one takes to reduce or "neutralize" risks. Hedging entails three steps: First, analyze the portfolio to identify and quantify risks and their sources. Second, in accord with a risk-management system, add, remove, and adjust holdings so that the risks are reduced or neutralized. Third, execute the trades necessary to implement the new portfolio. Sometimes hedging is as simple as selling part of the riskiest instruments in the portfolio, or adding a less-volatile one to it.

Single Trade Risk Management

Single-trade risk management can be summarized by these fundamental principles:

- Know how much one is willing to lose before he executes trade.

- See if the instrument is sufficiently liquid (active) so that one may buy or sell promptly.

- Determine the cut-loss level before trading.

- Determine the profit target (take-profit-level).

- Buy the contract only at an acceptable price level.

- If the trade starts to win significantly, raise the stop level so that the Winner Will Never Become a Loser.

- Take profit promptly as the trade reaches the profit target.

The risk management process has to start before one begins a trade. Most important, one must know beforehand how much one is willing to lose, along with how much one can lose in a planned trade. For example, before doing a trade, one should first consider potential losses, and decide if the stop-loss level is reasonable and acceptable.

Portfolio Risk Management

If one actively manages the risk of each trade in the portfolio, the whole-portfolio risk will be well under control. After all, a portfolio is just the aggregate of all individual single trades. However, it is also important to manage the overall risk at the portfolio level. The following is a list of key points for managing portfolio risk:

- Know the overall risk tolerance before building up the portfolio.

- Determine the overall cut-loss level.

- Diversify the investment in different stocks.

- Actively manage the risk of every individual trade.

- Know the overall risk and where the risk comes from.

- Act quickly when you see the risk limits exceeded.

- Close out the entire portfolio if it loses to the overall stop-loss level.

- Stay in the game.

This last point, "Stay in the game," is most important in trading and investing. It refers to cutting losses before they are too big. One can remain active by always recognizing risk limits in a trade, cutting losses and building profits.

Recent studies have shown that people don't tend to be rational economic actors; their decisions are based in part on their reactions to the facts at hand.

If one could always pick tops and bottoms, money management would not be needed. That is not possible though. Pretend a trading system was 99% accurate. The 1% failure rate could still wipe a trader out if he uses no money management. The 1% failure rate could be a loss that far exceeds the winners that you accumulate with the 99% accuracy ratio.

The risk-management strategies provide the crucial means of surviving and growing in today's market by applying the same rational controls that keep long-experienced traders ahead.

A fund experienced substantial trading losses in the first seven trading days that consumed nearly all of the fund's capital. These losses occurred principally in three position groups. The fund's portfolio was under liquidation and there was a strong possibility that there may not be any equity left at the end of the liquidation. The fund came into the year 2003 aggressively positioned in three trade groups. [1]

The fund held a significant position; it had a long position in a parent company and a short position in a 63%-owned subsidiary of the parent. The two stocks had exhibited a very high degree of correlation and low level of volatility. The underlying merits of the position were considered extremely attractive from both a valuation standpoint and a timing standpoint. In fact, the after-tax 63% position in the subsidiary was approximately equal to the market

---

[1] http://www.iht.com/articles/84633.html

value of the entire parent company so that by owning this position, one owned the parent company's valuable core business at minimal cost.

The fund's second position was a relative value position in the national bank sector, which consisted of long positions in three banks, a short position in one bank and some short index futures as a hedge. The position was established recently as some of the weaker national banks were heavily sold off in a market panic late in the year.

Third, the fund held a significant position in a national tech stock that had also been excessively sold off in the last quarter of the year. A large degree of panic selling was detected along with aggressive and large short sales of the stock.

The start it had was definitely not a good start at all. In the first two trading days the fund lost approximately 15% of its capital. This was very concerning as it immediately put the traders in a precarious margin position and forced them to consider unwinding positions to raise margin. The other concerning issue was that much of the adverse activity in their positions took place in the last half hour of trading each day.

While trying to raise cash in some of the fund's positions, the fund again sustained a loss of an additional 15% of its capital.

Unfortunately, the next day fund lost another 16% of it's capital. Once again, for the fourth day running, much of this loss occurred in the final hour of trading. After the close of the fourth day, prime brokers decided to exercise their right to supervise further trading/liquidation in the positions as per the standard prime brokerage agreement.

Attempts were then made to raise liquidity by selling positions. Traders did manage to work out of some size across the various positions, but the liquidation had the effect of further losses in the fund's positions. The fund ended the day down a further 12% and the week with a loss of approximately 58% of its capital. Eventually, in accordance with the prime brokerage agreement it was decided that they needed to liquidate the fund's two largest positions, the stub trade and the long tech position, as soon as possible. Various block trades cleared most of the exposure to the two positions but left the fund with a loss for the day of approximately 40%. Equity in the fund was now hovering at the 3% level.

Traders continued to sell out the relative value bank trade and clean up some smaller less liquid positions. They were left with very little equity in the fund, somewhere around 2% of start of year capital.

The fund still has positions that total approximately $80 million long and $117 million short. Of the long positions, approximately $15 million is held in lower liquidity stocks that may take some time to properly liquidate. They are still working hard with the prime broker to trade out of the remaining positions in as clean a fashion as possible.

Now let us identify the facts/errors made by the fund manager and take an account of things a trader should look at before venturing his capital:

- Having losses in 7 days that consume all capital is no risk control.

- Diversification limited to 3 markets is a ticking time bomb.

- Having 2 out of 3 positions highly correlated is no risk control.

- Value based trading & technical trading does not mix.

- Why buy into markets going straight down?

Money Management is also sometimes called asset allocation, position sizing, portfolio heat, portfolio allocation, cash flow management, trade management, capital management, position management, size management, bet size selection, lot size selection, or even Risk Control, Equity Control, and Damage Control. Money and risk management, plus diversification, are interwoven with trend trading. There are rather long periods in which no ascertainable trends can be seen in a given market. This period eventually passes and some trend manages to re-establish itself. Trend trading mandates that we wait for these periods to pass and not trade until a strong trend is observed.

'Money Management' deals with how to optimize capital usage and to view a portfolio as a whole. There are 2 steps to implement proper Money Management:

Bet sizing

The determination of what (fixed or non-fixed) fraction of a portfolio's total (or again fixed or non-fixed fraction) equity to risk on each trade expressed in denominated currency values.

Position sizing

Our money is at constant risk as well. No place is risk-free. The good news is that efficient Risk Management can turn risk into profit. It is about managing losses and open profits (unrealized trading returns) also the "process" of saving. The calculation of how many contracts should be held in a position, once a trade entry is signaled or the number of contracts/stocks that should not be traded in fractions and must be cut down to a whole integer is referred to as position sizing.

Position Trading and Risk Management

Protecting capital is important, but at the same time it is more important to know how to get good returns. *Smart Money* knows this and they act to earn greater profits.

Winning traders can only profit to the extent that other traders are willing to lose. Traders are willing to lose when they obtain external benefits from trading. The most important external benefits are expected returns from holding risky securities that represent deferred consumption. Hedging and gambling provide other external benefits. Markets would not exist without loosing traders. Their trading losses fund the winning traders who make prices efficient and provide liquidity. Controlling risk becomes extremely important while trading. Defy being a looser and the key to this is Risk Control.

Traders know that the key is risk control - if a trader controls his risks and runs his profits, he could position himself to make bigger money throughout the long term.

From previous Chapters we know that, wise investing adapts to different markets and different market conditions. The system is based on keeping things proportional to the market's volatility. During a volatile period, traders trade less contracts or shares. During periods of lower volatility, they trade more contracts or shares. In other words, commitments increase during favorable risk/reward periods and decrease during less favorable periods.

A volatility control is important for the psychological benefit. If there is too much volatility in any one position it attracts the attention of the trader. His focus shifts to one particular position as a result he may lose sight of the big picture. By controlling volatility risk exposure can be adjusted, keeping the trader psychologically balanced.

Basic Rules for Risk Control

The trader has to maintain some level of trading appropriate for the equity. Trading bases that could be measured are:

- Contracts
- Shares of stock
- Aggregate value
- Risk-to-stops
- Volatility

Equity can also measured as:

- Liquidation value of the account
- Liquidation value less risk

So a reader's job in our way of Investing is just to keep these well proportioned.

We have already established that Money and Portfolio management rules dictate the number of contracts or shares. We have also discussed precise formulas that set forth size. A trader who uses a constant trading size gives up an important edge in much the same way a blackjack player does when always betting the same regardless of what cards are on the table.

It can be said that common single contract/share measures of trading system performance such as win/loss ratio; percent winning trades, etc. are of little value to decision-making when using proper money/risk management. At the same time, identifying and following trends may be the only reasonable investment approach over the long term. Mechanical approach has more value as no scientific approach can be applied to discretionary trading. This is a methodology that would work through many market conditions. It is one of long-term approaches that work best over decades.

Our system has robust and adaptive parameters and it does not require re-optimization. The system uses indicators and parameters that adapt to changing market conditions.

The techniques outlined in this book, has periods of ups and downs in terms of performance. Once a reader begins Investing with proper portfolio and risk management, he will undoubtedly develop an equity curve. Once he has an equity curve, he can begin to trade it in such a fashion to reduce risk and enhance return. Let us understand how it is done.

In periods of losing (with the equity curve turning up), adding proportionally one additional position across markets is a good start. In periods of winning (with the equity curve turning down), subtracting proportionally one additional position across markets is a good start.

Traditionally, economic theory is based on the idea that market is rational and therefore makes rational decisions. Feelings and biases do not influence the investor's judgment, only relevant information affects their behavior. Decision-makers decide on basis of the probability of each alternative outcome and select the alternative giving the maximum return. This view is not supported without exception. In Risk Management a trader should avoid following making mistakes:

- Costs, that is, losses, made at an earlier time may predispose decision-makers to take risks.
- Situation framing also affects trader's decision.
- Negative games may cause a trader to go broke.
- A positive expectation means that the trader has an edge.
- Keeping what shows loss and selling what shows profit is one of the common mistakes committed by the trader.

The importance of cutting losses short is obvious. Large losses can be avoided if the trader only risks a small amount of capital in each and every trade and not letting a streak of losses compound into a big portion of initial capital.

When one enters the market, an expectation of winning that is positive must be present. To enter the market without a market expectation or a negative expectation is to lose money. One should feel comfortable wagering money with this positive expectation.

Risk Control – Break-even facts

- A loss of 2% requires a gain of 3% on remaining capital in order to break even.

- A loss of 30% requires a gain of 43% on remaining capital in order to break even.

- A loss of 50% requires a gain of 100% on remaining capital in order to break even.

- A loss of 90% requires a gain of 1000% on remaining capital in order to break even.

Streaks/Gamblers Fallacy: When probability of winning is 50%, then there will be an equal number of wins and losses over a large number of draws. A common misconception is that a winner will follow after a loser has been drawn.

Prospect theory/Disposition Effects:

Psychological research has found that most individuals are risk seeking when the situation at hand is perceived as a losing situation and risk-averse when the situation is perceived as a winning situation.

R – multiples: The losing trades should be small R-multiples and the winning trades large R-multiples. A low "hit-rate" (probability of winning/losing) with large winners and small losers (e.g. 10R winners and 1R losers) is preferable to a high probability of winning with small winners and big losers.

Computing: A basic knowledge of computing the possibility of a certain gain is essential.

There are several alternate methods that can be used for managing risk;

- New Position Risk

- Ongoing Risk Exposure

- Daily Volatility

The key is reliance on volatility and account size in determining the proper portfolio to trade.

Analyzing Size, Risk/Reward Ratio, And Percent Accuracy

As stated earlier in the money management chapter, choices made are influenced by how a situation is framed. As a consequence, there is greater risk and gamble in a losing situation, holding on to the position in hope that prices will recover. In a winning situation the circumstances are reversed. Investors will become risk averse and quickly take profits, not letting profits run.

The Position Trading speculators hunts for the outsized large move; a few big trades make up the bulk of profits and many small trades make up the losses. Winning trades can range from 35-50%, but that percentage reveals little information since we expect more losses (of smaller value) than winners (of much larger value). Win/loss ratio, while a favorite of the novice trader, is useless in terms of our analysis. *Smart Money* uses a 2% money management stop on each position they take, so they limit risk to 2% of their capital. The concept of the Speculators sitting out the next signal if the prior position was a winner is an important aspect of the entry signal process. If the last trade within the system was a loss, initiation at the current signal has more positive mathematical expectation. Even if the last trade was a loss on a short position, the next signal, even if it is a long signal, still has greater expectation.

Units are constantly adjusted based on account equity. Later we shall explain how money management *units* allow an easy way to manage risk and control equity.

How to Use Risk Management to Ensure no Blowouts

The need for professional risk and money management techniques is a foundation for success. In an age where it has become fashionable to manage one's own investments, very few traders have implemented disciplined, professional money management strategies.

Speculators view their portfolios as a whole and optimize capital usage. They move from a defensive or reactive view of risk in which the risk is measured to avoid losses, to an offensive or proactive posture in which risks are actively managed for a more efficient use of capital.

Money management determines how many shares or contracts to trade. This is the most crucial concern a trader faces; it determines risk and profit. It is a defensive concept that keeps a trader in the game to play another day. For example, money management would tell whether there is enough new money to trade additional positions. However, money management would not focus on stop placement, as some mistakenly believe. Stop placement does not address the "how much question".

Position Trading is grounded in a system of risk control and money management. The math is straightforward and easy to learn. During periods of higher market volatility, trading size is reduced. During losing periods, positions are reduced and trade size is cut back. The main objective is to preserve capital until more favorable price trends reappear. In this chapter we will understand how the system determines crucial decisions such as:

- How and when to enter the market

- How many contracts or shares to trade at any time

- How much money to risk on each trade

- How to exit the trade if it becomes unprofitable

- How to exit the trade if it becomes profitable

This section of the chapter will address the questions mentioned above.

Risk level among trend-followers varies depending upon the size of the profit they seek. For example, if 100%+ a year gains are sought, then one must be prepared for the possibility of a 30%. The long term Speculators search for the outsized large move. Several big trends a year are key to success. The strategy cuts the losing positions quickly. Consequently, a few big trades make up the bulk of the profits and many small trades make up the losses. Winning trades can range from 35-50%, but that percentage reveals little information since more losses (of smaller value) than winners (of much larger value) is expected. Win/loss ratio is useless in terms of our analysis. Besides this, Position Trading system also deals with volatility. The real risk on any trade is 2% of the original capital risked on that particular trade. Controlling the real risk and the risk that follows is an absolute foundation of money management.

The approach described below is simplistic but effective. One should rely on the market to dictate the level of exposure at any point of time. Typically, as trading activity becomes volatile, the margin requirements increase. At that time, one should reduce the exposure because only a 1 percent commitment would have been specifically allocated to that market for this particular market timing method. Conversely, when price activity becomes inactive and less volatile, one should increase the investment exposure, hopefully, awaiting a breakout and increased volatility. Consequently, margin requirements serve as a barometer for fund allocation. So whenever margin requirements are raised, market exposure as measured by the number of contracts traded should be adjusted accordingly.

Example:
Portfolio size = $100,000
3 trading systems with the limitation of trading only 10 markets in each.

The maximum exposure can be no greater than $300,000 dollars, since that amount accounts for 30 percent of $1 million.

Therefore, each market represents $10,000 dollars. If the margin requirement in one market is $1,000, then 10 contracts could be traded at any one time. If volatility increases, the exchange may decide to raise margin requirements by an additional $1,000 to $2,000, thereby forcing to reduce the position size to five contracts (5 x 2,000 = $10,000 and 10 x $1,000 = $10,000).

What has effectively occurred is a portfolio contract-size adjustment of 50 percent due to a 100 percent increase in margin requirements. If the trader is still positioned in the market even though the volatility has increased sufficiently and the exchange has raised the margin requirements, it is likely that the market has moved in his favor. The initial exposure was a function of margin requirements, and the change was made as a result of market volatility and potential risk as defined by the increase in margin requirements. Generally, funds do not risk any more than 2% of the portfolio on any one trade, but once in a trade, stop losses must be introduced. If he desires to increase this stop loss, the size of the position or exposure in that market at that particular time should be reduced accordingly.

As the portfolio size in one method and in one market increases, traders should adjust their stop loss and profit-taking levels and make certain that their exposure does not constitute an undue weighting in the portfolio. In fact, as the profit in a position increases, traders should reduce the position size to maintain a maximum portfolio exposure and, ideally, in effect they will be investing only the profits generated in the trade.

While winning Speculators experience a lot of volatility, it is concentrated on the upside, not the downside. This demonstrates clearly that *smart money* cut their losses and let their profits run.

Our system has no price predictions; positions that are scaled to a portfolio's size; obsessive attention to profit-to-loss ratios, money management and the risk of ruin - all in pursuit of capturing gains from trends that are historically certain to appear.

Price movement is predominantly random. The secret is to make money in the market, which is not random, and exploiting it to the fullest.

First law of price movement is:
- If prices move up there is greater probability they will move higher rather than lower.

- If prices move down there is greater probability that they will move lower rather than higher.

Second law of price movement is:
- If price goes up one must buy the market long and if price goes down then one must sell the market short.

Speculators sell what shows a loss and keep what shows a profit. This is only the wise thing to do. Generally, traders end up doing just the reverse. Investors and traders, shifting in risk tolerance according to positively and negatively framed situations, show no risk aversion, but an aversion against losses. Loss aversion applies when one is avoiding a loss even if it means accepting a higher risk. The preference for risky actions to avoid an impending loss over less risky options just to minimize the loss and "bite the bullet" can be explained by "loss aversion".

Many investors ride the trend. Unfortunately, most of them have no exit plan. So, when the market starts dropping they hold on. Nothing but a loss tells when one is making wrong decisions regarding trade. A loss is a clue to take action instead of simply avoiding mistake. There are rules that get a trader out. Even worse than taking no action when faced with losses is buying more because the lower price seems like a good value. Investors start focusing on the break-even levels. They start worrying about getting back to where they were. Unless the first loss is made, one will continue to lose.

Consequently, a few big trades make up the bulk of the profits and many small trades make up all the losses. Winning trades may range from 35-50%, but that percentage reveals little information since more losses (of smaller value) are expected than winners (of much larger value). Win/loss ratio is may be a favorite of the novice trader, but it should be remembered that it is useless in Position Trading.

Stop and Reverse method

The method involves utilizing some kind of indicator preferably price based. If the system is long one contract and the market comes back and the price is hit, the system sells 2 contracts and reverses to a short position and so on.

Trailing Stop

The idea behind a trailing stop is that it allows "profits to run" while at the same time "locking in" any profits already made. The problem is that if the trailing stop is too tight it results in stop right before the start of a big move. On the contrary if the stop is too deep it results in many small profits going to large losses. With a trailing stop the profits are taken only after the market has turned against. This results in frequently being forced to sell out long position when many others are trying to sell too.

Adjust Trading on a Win or Loss Technique

Pyramiding (up and down) as we call it and Martingale (normal and reverse). It consists of varying the number of units/contracts taken and is based upon the results of the last trade. For example, traders can choose to double up on a position after a losing trade in hopes of recouping losses or doubling up only after a winning trade to maximize the system's potential. This can be a very effective money management technique/strategy.

The main strength of this technique is that it allows traders to maximize the risk reward ratio on high probability opportunities, while reducing the risk on low probability situations. The result is that a trading account can grow substantially faster, without increasing the over all risk to it. It is relatively easy to implement in real time. Once traders are aware of the desired pyramiding technique to use, it is easy for them to know exactly how many positions to take on the next trade, based on the results of the last trade.

Crossing Equity Curves Technique

This technique minimizes the drawdown periods and can actually improve the percentage of winning trades taken. Traders usually use two moving averages to enter the market when the short moving average crosses the larger moving average. They would enter a long position when the short average crosses from below to above the longer moving average, and vice a versa for a short position. First, an average of the profit of all the trades is decided on a long and short moving average. The shorter average is an average of the profit (or loss) and longer average is an average of a lager block of the most recent trades. When the short average is greater than the long average, it means the trading system is doing better per trade than it has done in the immediate past. If the short average is less than the long average, it means the trading system is doing worse now than it did in the immediate past, on a per trade basis. It is reasoned that this strategy will help keep traders out of long periods. Additionally, traders will only be trading the system when it is "in sync" with the markets. Numerous results show this to be true. Often, traders can achieve equal or greater profit, with fewer drawdowns, on fewer trades. The fact that a higher profit is achieved on fewer trades is an especially attractive bonus. Fewer trades result in fewer fixed costs and less exposure to the market.

Optimal f Technique

This technique finds the most favorable amount to risk on each trading opportunity. Trading with this optimal amount of capital results in the greatest gain to the account. If traders risk either a higher or lower dollar amount, they will make less money. It is important to note that any time traders are risking more than the optimal value, they are getting less return on their money with a greater risk to their account. It is because of this drawdown value that traders may not want to trade their accounts at the optimal level.

Z-score

The Z-score, helps analyzing the dependence between trades, is calculated by comparing the number of runs there are in a set of trades, with the number of runs that would be expected statistically. This number is then usually transformed into another value called the Confidence limit. The Confidence limit is expressed in terms of a percentage. The calculations relying on the standard deviation of the system, for example, one standard deviation represents the area where 68% of all the events will fall. If the Z-score were one then the confidence limit would be 68%.

The Z-score can be either positive or negative. A negative Z-score means there are fewer streaks in the sample of trades tested than would be expected statistically. On the other hand, a positive Z-score means there are more streaks in the trading system than would be expected. This means winning trades tend to follow losing trades and vice a versa.

If traders find a system with a reasonable Confidence level, it is possible to exploit this aspect of the system.

Probability of Ruin

The Probability of Ruin (POR) is the "statistical possibility" a trading system will deplete an account to the point of ruin, before achieving a dollar level deemed as being successful. Ruin is defined as the level of an account when traders will stop trading. Knowing this value can be very important to traders. The POR illustrates to traders the statistical possibility that their trading systems will naturally, by the laws of probability, drift to a point of success or ruin.

To calculate the Probability of Ruin, all other things being equal:

- The greater the size of the average wins, the lower the POR

- The larger the average risk per trade, the greater the POR

- The larger the initial account size, the lower the POR

- The higher the percentage of winning trades, the lower the POR

- The smaller the account, the greater the POR

Position Trading is 100 per cent systematized in a mechanical manner. Price and time are essential at all times because one cannot tell how the market is going to move, also because fundamentals often turn out to be media hype or stale data. Prices fluctuate due to underlying economic activities that is learnt about in hindsight. There are so many variables, most of them hidden. If the Investment program works, it's not because it can predict the trend but because it can react to it.

How To Take a Loss To Avoid Larger Losses

Watching the hard-earned capital disappear is never a pleasant experience. Most people quit trading after their first four or five losses. It is true that novice traders don't like to think about setting a stop-loss because it reminds them of this potential negative consequence. After a loss is made, one is more likely to receive a "blinding flash of the obvious". This revelation can drive improvements into his trading plan. Traders should recognize that by planning for every contingency, the chance of sustained success increases.

If self-esteem is tied to whether one is making profit while trading, then he is due to have a short career as a trader. Smart speculators are taught to remember always that a person is not a "loser" if he makes a loss, he is only a "loser" if he doesn't follow written trading plan.

The first aim must be capital preservation. Systematically getting out of the loosing trade is the key. Without a clear idea regarding how to set a stop-loss, a trader's longevity as a trader is limited. To effectively do this for options and warrants, one needs to access real-time price data. If a trader depletes his capital to the point that he can no longer trade effectively, then he will never know what could have been. Making money is a by-product of following trading rules. Following a sound stop-loss strategy is an essential skill.

For example, in 2000 Tech stocks went straight down. Prices down by 50% were definitely a loss signal. Most people held their investments assuming that they would bounce back up, but it sank from being down only 50% to drop to 95% down.

Risk Controlling is also crucial because losses determine what to do right. General Atlantic Partners (GAP), a venture capital firm was a 10% owner in Price line. GAP had a system for deciding that the time was right to exit a substantial portion of their Price line position, so early in the year GAP sold 4,946,029 shares of Price line for $278,510,893 ($56.31/share). They made a killing and now Price line is all but worthless, currently down from its 52 week high by 95%.

Smart traders handle loss by limiting all positions to a set percent of equity. If equity is going down due to losses, one should decrease trading size. On the other hand when going up, one should automatically compound profits and add more.

Types of stops

An initial stop is designed to protect the capital. Even successful traders find that they make only winning trades around 50 per cent of the time. As long as the dollars gained outweigh the dollars lost, one will be profitable, even if the hit-rate is low.

If a trader enters a trade and almost immediately it changes direction - then he need to exit. For leveraged instruments such as options and warrants, a "hard dollar stop" can work effectively. When one has lost 2% of the allocated trading equity in any particular trade, he should exit that position immediately.

A break-even stop will help lock in a no-loss trade. This type of stop is implemented once a trade has begun to co-operate and there is now little threat of the initial stop being hit. It's always a great feeling when one can move the stop to cover the costs of the transaction. At least when one has moved the stop to break-even, there is a chance that he will end up with a profitable trade. Especially with the application of leverage, it is important to move the stop to break-even as soon as reasonably possible. This will minimize the potential drawdown of the account.

Trailing stops are designed to protect profits. Once the trade has trended strongly in the expected direction, one can follow the trend by moving stop. One could also decide to extract money from the position if the option hits profit target. In leveraged, volatile trades, however, profits can quickly turn into losses, so extracting some money at significant benchmarks makes sense. *Smart money* protects profits as well as initial capital to trading effectively.

Traders may also need to consider a time stop if the instrument doesn't co-operate in the allotted time frame. Due to the effect of time decay on options and warrants, it is essential to set a time stop, or it is guaranteed that they will lose all of their trading equity in that position.

Try not to be too trigger happy when exiting based on a time stop for a share. The markets distribute money from the impatient to the patient. Give the trade a chance to co-operate before exiting.

How to set stops

There are four main ways to set a stop-loss:

Pattern-based stop-loss

In a pattern-based stop loss traders exit trades when the share breaks downwards through a trend line.

Using Technical Indicators

Traders can make a stop using Technical indicators. An example can be, a dead cross of two moving averages may trigger an exit.

Percent methods

Traders make an exit when the instrument drops in value by a set percentage.

Volatility-based stops

For an exit from the trade traders rely on significant changes in volatility past a pre-defined level.

The risk can be estimated as the drop from entry point to exit point, that is, the difference between actual buying price and predetermined selling price multiplied by the number of shares sold. When the market moves against the trader's position and he decides it is time to close the trade, the price movement multiplied by position size determines the size of the loss. Following this reasoning, the potential profit that one can receive depends on price rise and position size. When a loss is realized there is an obvious mathematical rule regarding drawdowns affecting recovery. If losing $1,000 out of a total of $10,000 (a 10%-loss), then to get even, there is a need of 11.1% increase on the remaining $9,000. The larger the loss, the greater profit must be obtained to recover. A 30% loss requires a profit on remaining capital of 43%. The importance of cutting losses short is quite logical. If the trader is unable to survive in the markets on a near term basis, then he will not be around when opportunities arise to make money on the long term.

Whenever in a losing trade, one would like to get out but it can get difficult if the liquidity isn't there. In the bond market, because of the liquidity factor and the way it trades, traders will be able to execute trades at better prices than if he is emotional about it. And very importantly, one should pick spot where getting out of the trade is easy.

So the emphasis should be directed toward maximizing gains, two concepts of position-sizing strategies are "letting the profits run" and "cutting losses short". Besides these two concepts, having a high percentage of winning trades and being able to pick the "right" stock or ignoring a losing trade is also important while trading.

Loss control

Consider that a trader has $5000 to trade, and he looses 50% of this amount. How much money in percentage terms is left to make to break-even on the next trade? If the answer is 50%, it's a wrong answer. The trader would require making 100% on the remaining $2500, to make up the lost $2500, and break-even. If this amount is again lost, then he must make 33.3% profit on the remaining equity, simply to break-even. This is a tricky proposition. The trader, in such a scenario, should keep the total equity to less than 20%, and then there is a chance of surviving in the share market. Remember - trading is not about avoiding risk; it is about managing risk. The golden rule of trading is to keep the losses small and let the profits run. Stop-losses provide a sign that it is time to exit position, as the trade is no longer co-operating with the initial view. Most good trading plans capital allocate a maximum of 15-20 per cent for trading speculative shares, options and warrants. This is another way that one can minimize the risk of a monumental loss.

How To Trade for Both Long and Short Positions

Short term trading is not, by definition, less risky. Some people may mistakenly apply a cause and effect relationship between using a long-term strategy and the potential of incurring large loss. They forget profit and loss is proportional. A short-term system will never allow to be in the trend long enough to achieve large profits. A trader may end up with small losses but also small profits. Added together, numerous small losses equal a big loss.

When trading for the long term, the trader has a more positive expectation in terms of the size of the move. In the big picture, the larger the move, the larger the validation of the move.

If trading some short-term pattern predictive system a trader would never be able to participate fully in the big trends. Big trends make the big profits. Position Trading for the long-term places far less emphasis on perfect fills for success. In contrast, short term traders' transaction costs and skids on their fills affect their bottom line to a much greater degree. On the other hand to compensate for profit roll-off, short-term traders have to be very good guessers. To improve guessing skills, one can practice dealing cards from a standard deck. One might be able to make money with short term trading if practiced well.

When trading options in a way that capitalizes on "time decay", one would expect to win often, but not win much. Many new options traders figure that the occasional thousand percent win will be enough to compensate for all the losses on their trades when the things expire worthless, but for most options traders the reality is that this is the death of a thousand cuts. One would so severely on the capital (after commissions are taken into account) that in all probability one may have great difficulty climbing out even when one finally get a big win.

Smart Investors make money going both long and short. It makes no difference what a company actually does. Trade the price up or down with a mechanical system.

When most people first start trading they often start small. As they get better at it, they trade more. They might start with one contract and then move to ten contracts. As time progresses, they reach a certain comfort level with their trading, but are still afraid to take risks beyond that level. As a result, they never trade at levels of 100 contracts or 1,000, so they never experience large profits. There is a better way in which the object is to try to keep things in constant leverage terms. In other words, one should trade the same as the equity increases. By using our approach to money management, one should be confident of getting big.

Risk taking is essential to successful trading, as long as it is calculated risk. When a risk is taken it is useful to have a mechanical trading system for several reasons: increased diversification, reduced workload and thereby making trading life easier.

Mechanical trading systems enable a trader to take a risk without getting personally involved. Although one might not be happy when going through or taking a loss, at least that is better than agonizing over trading decisions on a day-to-day basis. It's the rare individual who can sit in front of a quote screen and make consistently good trading decisions day after day. Other components of life will always impact thinking generally and trading decisions specifically, unless one rely on a mechanical system.

Position Trading trading is predicated on the fact that human beings are not psychologically equipped to interact profitably with markets. When money is involved, psychological pulls interfere with objectivity. As a result, human beings who have money on the line tend to take their losses too late and their profits too soon. The problem of taking profits too soon particularly affects traders. They often feel a strong desire to close out a profitable position when it starts to move against them. Mechanical systems overcome these psychological and emotional reactions.

Position trading is trading on a longer time frame than day trading. Instead of minutes or hours one holds for several weeks or months. The line between trading and more basic speculation here is blurred because it is hard to tell a position trader apart from someone who doesn't know the difference between investment and speculation and thus has a very high portfolio turnover.

Most successful traders are position traders. They may hold for many months and take substantial profits at the end, though of course if they are trading to limit risk they will be ready to eliminate any stock or contract from their portfolio that starts to turn down.

After trading for a while, keeping trade size small at first, one will have capital available when the analysis is done and one will know what sort of statistics the trading style produces. This is one good reason why many gurus tell to stick with the system and not change it on a whim. A trader needs to understand not just the market, but also himself - because the method is part of him, it comes from his educational background and psychology.

Smart Money never adds to a losing position, they add mechanically to winning positions. And they only add to winning positions when they can do so without substantially adding risk to original capital. Therefore one can be wrong several times and right once, and still perform well.

The alternative would be to keep the position size same as on a winning position, which means one has to be right substantially more often, and would have to allow position to go much further. Traders desire that winning positions be far more dynamic than losing ones.

A basic trading strategy for many Position Traders is to hold positions (either long or short) with the major price trend of each stock or future in a portfolio. This approach is designed to capture a substantial fraction of the total profit potential from important changes in an instrument's price. Smart traders do not try to predict when the next important move will occur. They do not try to forecast when a particular market will enter a choppy and unprofitable trading phase. Position Trading will contain the inevitable series of small losses and whipsaws within tolerable limits, but position the trader to benefit from major price trends whenever they develop. The decisions necessary to implement Position Trading strategies are derived from the price.

The time constant of a system determines the type of trend to which it responds, short-term or long-term.

A short-term system tends to deliver lots of quick trades while a long-term system tends to deliver fewer slow trades. Both types of system can deliver strings of winners and losers.

Simulations can reveal the characteristic performance of a system over time, and can help the trader to design risk management strategies so as to place the volatility within the range of his own psychological stamina.

During trend markets, while trends continue smoothly, most trend systems tend to register profits. Risk management is for the rest of the time.

Our rules typically allow only 10 units to be put on at any one time. However, 10 long positions and 10 short positions are considered less risk than an outright 10 long or 10 short positions. As a result, an ideal portfolio would be 10 long and 10 short.

Savvy investors have discovered that due to the exponential nature of bull markets, short positions were only 75% as profitable as long positions. This, however, does not imply that one should not trade short positions, but must be able to trade short as easily as long trade.

Managing portfolio is an important aspect of Position Trading System. It rejects the Buy and Hold approach as outdated and irrational. It should always be remembered that there are clear effective strategies that one can use to exit markets at proper times that enhance profitability.

Stay Within The Portfolio Risk Parameters

When trading like *Smart Money*, it should be thoroughly understood that the risk taken per trade and the profit target should not be just any dollar amount. Risks taken should be based on the current volatility of the market. The reason behind this is, Smart Money let the market show them a predefined percentage of new equity before they can add on more units.

We already know that the strength of Position Trading system is pyramiding and allowance of proper diversification. With units calculated across different contracts, *Smart Money* can always maintain a proper risk parameter even if volatility changes overnight. Diversification is important because Smart Money make most of their money in 30 percent of their trades. When we may not have a meaningful trend in the stock market, another trade for example: oil or currencies can be trending very nicely. Therefore, Smart Money doesn't just watch one market; they watch any trend in all markets. They take many small losses of 1-2% but take geometric gains when they catch a big trend and pyramid it correctly.

Even when following all major trends in the market, it is sometimes crucial to choose the markets to be traded. As per few traders, liquid markets exhibit consistency over time and are also less risky. To trade successfully the redemption should be at hand, so it is always recommended to trade liquid markets.

Talking about Trade entry, it contributes about 20% to trading success. Trend-followers consider that getting aboard a trend at an early stage is best suited for trade entry. They believe that it is important to trade with the trend irrespective of entering a trend on a breakout or a moving average crossover or having a more exotic approach. Most traders have an intuitive grasp of risk and the importance of diversifying their portfolios by time (short-term vs. long-term holdings), asset class (stocks, bonds and money market instruments), and securities (avoiding concentrated positions in any single holding) and sectors. They avoid putting all their investment eggs in one basket.

Statistician's term "Investment Correlation" is the answer for why shouldn't they put all their investment eggs in one basket. Let us understand this with a macro level example, a trader has a broadly diversified portfolio across the U.S. stock market. If a broad economic slowdown or recession hits, most of his holdings are likely to decline in price. The greatest risk any portfolio faces is that closely related developments or economic forces might affect the investments that compose it.

While the well-balanced portfolio should provide the most consistent returns, how one goes about achieving this depends on where he is in the investment spectrum. If the client is starting off an investment portfolio and hopes to add to it over the years, then he should really start off with a mainstream fund as a core holding. If he has a fairly mature investment portfolio, it will be easier to achieve better diversification even if it means reorganizing what he has. A starting point as a model growth portfolio would therefore be for the investor to use a growth portfolio as a base and either make it more aggressive or less aggressive by the use of funds and capital allocation.

By combining assets that are not strongly correlated and by Fund Switching, Position Trading maintains overall portfolio returns while reducing portfolio risk.

Set stops

- First we determine how much risk can be taken.

- They sell until comfortable with the size.

- We do not trade considering what others have to say.

- It should always be remembered that just because a stock is down a lot doesn't mean it's a good bargain.

- Smart money always buys with a meaningful size.

How To Handle the Risk of Ruin

Now that we have understood the concept of risk in trading markets, what could probably be Risk of Ruin? It is simply described, as the chance of losing so much that one must stop trading. The insuperable mantra to check this is to specify the maximum amount one is willing to lose, constituting ruin and then adjusting accordingly. It is understood that, once profits accumulate, the chance of ruin decreases. In other words, the greatest risk is at the beginning of any trade.

In Trend-follower style success, understanding risk of ruin is very crucial. Unlike other trading systems, Position Trading is a mechanical, statistical method of looking at probabilities and use risk of ruin concepts to adjust their unit size based on fluctuations in the account. As one gains in account size he would need to consider False Ruin. For example, if a trader gets to 200%, he should think of 130%.

Ruin will need to be adjusted accordingly to bankroll. An example would be, given:
Equity drops 25%
Trader has a 1 ATR expectation
No reduction in trading size then
There is a 20% chance of blowing out.
However, if you reduce trading size there is a 14% chance of blowing out.

Risk of ruin (ROR) can also be used to estimate whether or not a system is suitable for a trader to trade. Say for example the original capital - one of the factors that influence risk of ruin. A trader might not have enough money to trade like well-funded investors successfully based on a probable estimate of maximum drawdowns etc. Consequently, ROR might not help him developing the ultimate trading system, but it will provide a theoretical rating of any system he is considering to trade.

Based on a trader's trading statistics, it is possible to make an estimate of risk of ruin. Symmetric risk of ruin (RoR) = $((1 - P) / (1 + P))/x$. Where P is the probability of winning on any trade and; x is the proportion of the account that is risked on any given trade. Looking at the proportion of winning trades/bets one makes one can figure out P, x is entirely voluntary. Also the risk of ruin increases greatly when the bets are big. The formula is also known as the "symmetric risk of ruin", as it assumes that a trader makes as much money on each winning trade as he loses on each losing trade. The actual amount won or lost per bet doesn't matter, just that the upside is the same as the downside, i.e. it is "symmetric". An intelligent trader should always remember that all good traders are not in the business to try to make a bundle on each and every trade. They try to maximize their winning trades but they do this by holding onto winners throughout trends, not by making huge bets because they are confident in their own forecasting abilities. This underpins the concept of trading like Smart Money.

As many traders know, success depends as much on money management strategy as it does on a particular trading system. Optimal f and Probability Of Ruin (POR) are two key money management concepts that help determining how to best allocate capital for maximum growth and minimal risk to the account.

The POR is the likelihood that the system will reach a point of success or failure. In other words the chance that one will blow out his account before hitting his financial goal. Ruin is defined as the account level at which a trader stops trading. The POR is calculated using the percentage win, the average wins, the average loss, the account size, the account size at ruin and the account size at success. The probability of ruin increases with the amount risked, so it is important that a trader limits the amount of capital committed to each trade. By trading smaller portions of the account equity, there is a greater chance a well-tested system will perform closer to its historical results. Traders who risk a larger percentage of account equity are more susceptible to variation from the expected results because of the small trade sample size.

Optimal f and POR calculations do not always suggest the same risk parameters. By comparing optimal f and POR, one can determine if the amount of capital risked at the optimal f value results in an unacceptably high POR. On the other hand, a trader may wish to increase the POR for the chance of exponentially higher returns. Ultimately this is a decision every trader must make. The optimal f amount suggests how much to risk; the POR value gives an idea of the relative risk associated with trading this amount.

Conclusion

Winning and loosing are as natural as breathing in and breathing out. Traders who can celebrate both winning and losing as a natural process can also buy and sell the same way. We would like to conclude this unit by reviewing the mistakes of the best and brightest with the aim that these can be avoided by a more intelligent trader. These mistakes include:

- Not diversifying because they know they are right

Smart people have multiple degrees and have been good throughout their academic lives. Smart people know they are smart because people tell them so. If all this is taken on head, it can prove to be very perilous. Therefore, there is one thing that a trader should always remember: They cannot outsmart the market.

- Not using a sell strategy

Trader's who know that they have stacked the odds in their favor and have done their homework are actually most ill prepared. As this assures them that they cannot fail. Who needs a sell strategy when one knows he is right? To be noticed is that the market has ways of proving people wrong.

- Averaging down in a losing position

Smart people know the investment idea was good before, so it's an even better deal now if one can buy in cheaper, right? Wrong. The concept is wrong because the market can continue lower. Investing further in a losing position can severely beat up a portfolio and sometimes put investors out of the game. Past performance does not predict future results. Smart people sometimes think that, by taking vast sums of data and analyzing it extensively, they have an edge in predicting what the market will do next. Blowups will occur when the market does something it has never done before.

- Over-optimizing a strategy using historical data

Smart traders may consider countless parameter sets in their strategies to trade, with only one problem. The problem is it generally seems like they are fighting the last battle in the markets in their simulations, not necessarily the next one that they should be concentrating on. They don't give themselves sufficient what-if scenarios that might occur and don't prepare for the what-ifs properly.

- Searching for perfection

Intelligent traders can come up with so many potentially better ways to trade that they sometimes spend most of their lives searching for perfection. Often the better approach is trading the best strategy they have at the moment and realizing they can work at making it better over the long run.

Frequently changing an existing losing trading strategy to a better strategy

Smart people often have very active minds that can dream up all sorts of new, better ways to trade. Some ways even can be quite complicated to satisfy their intellectual firepower. The strategy that looks hot right now may become cold down the road and this year's mediocre strategy may become next year's star performer. Position Traders do not have to deal with, and cannot deal with possible crashes, since they do not exist in the present.

Extreme market trends can appear from out of nowhere moving either up or down. These trends often feed upon themselves and can quickly progress geometrically allowing an opportunity for huge profits if a trader got into the trend early with a plan. However, to appreciate why market trends, or epidemics, can be so powerfully rewarding there can be no expectation of proportionality. People may be afraid to work with this type of progression, because the end result so often seems out of all proportion to the cause. The progression takes on a life of its own that may seem out of control and irrational. With Position Trading, there is always the possibility that big market changes may follow extremely small events, or that a change can happen very quickly. The appreciation of geometric progressions comes from understanding and being prepared for them. Position Trading trading is designed to find and exploit those market trends long before they arrive on the radar screen of the masses.

The essence of risk management: Risk no more than you can afford to lose, and also risk enough so that a win is meaningful. If there is no such amount, don't play.

Asset Allocation

Why do investors focus only either Real Estate of the stock markets? Partial explanation could be lack of funds to diversify properly.

Investors may also limit the number of vehicles in their portfolios may be due to search and monitoring costs and may develop a false perception that they can manage their portfolio risks better by a thorough understanding of a small number of securities rather than diversifying.

Lack of diversification may also result from psychological factors, in particular, due to an "illusion of control". It has been observed that when factors such as involvement, choice and familiarity are introduced into situations that may turn "by chance", people gain confidence and they start to believe that they can control the outcome of chance events. Investors may develop an illusory sense of control because in such situations they make their own choices instead of relying on others for their investment decisions.

Familiarity with a certain set of stocks may further worsen the illusion of control. In such cases, again, the investors may fail to realize that more knowledge or more information does not necessarily results in control over the outcome.

Result? Investors have a strong tendency to invest in stocks that they are familiar with. An illusion of control creates an unsuitable level of overconfidence. Further, investors may mistakenly believe that they can repeat success over and over by active trading and consequently they may choose not to diversify.

Why is Diversification Necessary?

All investors should realize that the major benefit of portfolio diversification is the potential to increase returns in the long term through minimizing risk and reducing the negative effects of market volatility on the portfolio. Investing globally and spreading risk across a variety of investments are strong diversification strategies. Both these strategies can play a vital part in realizing long-term financial goals.

There are several other ways to potentially maximize the value of the portfolio over the long term. One of these is to allocate money among various types of investments, such as stocks, bonds, money market instruments or mutual funds. A study among pension fund managers showed that more than 91% of a portfolio's returns depends not on specific stocks, bonds or mutual funds selected, but on how the money is allocated among different types of investments. [1]

In spite of the fact that improved diversification does not indicate improvements in investors' stock selection abilities, it does have a considerable impact on investors' portfolio performance. Over time, the risk-adjusted performance of investor's portfolios increases across portfolios of all sizes. Improved diversification also influences the composition of the aggregate investor portfolio. There is a clear shift in the composition of the aggregate portfolio from small to large and from value to growth stocks. The risk level of investor portfolios decreases and the magnitude of performance increase over time.

It is possible that investors do not diversify appropriately due to the small size of their portfolio. The inability of investors to buy in round lots and overall higher stock prices may prevent investors with smaller portfolios from diversifying. Clearly, investors holding larger portfolios are more diversified and earn higher risk-adjusted performance but there is no evidence that investors holding a larger number of stocks are able to reduce the variance of their portfolios through better stock selection. The average correlation among stocks in portfolios containing a larger number of stocks is not lower than the average correlation among stocks in portfolios with fewer stocks. This indicates that investors with larger portfolios have better diversified portfolios merely because they hold a larger number of stocks and not due to any inherent superior portfolio composition skills.

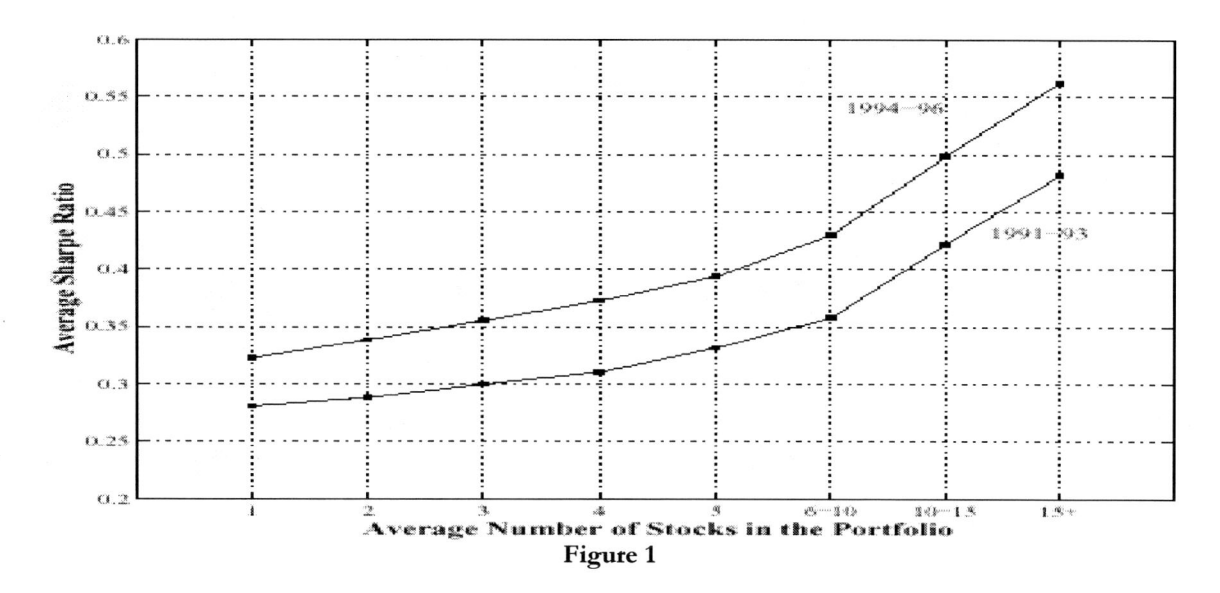

Figure 1

The figure shows the relationship between portfolio diversification (measured using the average number of stocks in the portfolio) and risk-adjusted portfolio performance (measured using Sharpe Ratio). The chart shows that in the 1994-96 sub-period, the average SR for 2-stock portfolios is 0.34 while portfolios with 15 or more stocks, on average, earn a SR of 0.56. It is evident from the plot that the strong positive relation between diversification and performance is present in each of the two 3-year sub-periods. There is also an improvement in risk-adjusted performance over time — SR during the second 3-year sub-period (1994-96) is considerably higher than the SR during the first 3-year sub-period (1991-93). This performance improvement is evident across portfolios of all sizes. Overall, these results suggest that better diversification translates into better risk-adjusted performance. However, investors may be able to achieve these levels of risk-adjusted performance by simply investing in one of the many available index funds. Similar results are obtained if other measures of diversification are used.

---

[1] (Source: "Determinants of Portfolio Performance II: An Update," Financial Analysts Journal, May/June, 1991. Based on data collected from 82 pension plans from 1977-1987.)

There is a strong positive relation between the degree of diversification and portfolio performance — better diversified portfolios earn higher risk-adjusted returns.

Another possibility is that investors who are less diversified hold stocks with lower volatility - they may disregard correlations among stocks and mistakenly believe that a collection of lower volatility stocks leads to a less risky portfolio. In fact, less diversified investors hold more volatile stocks. (More on this later in the chapter)

In sum, it is suggested that investors are unable to (or unwilling to) choose stocks in a in a manner consistent with the goal of diversification. They appear to adopt a "naive" diversification strategy where they hold portfolios with several stocks but do not give proper consideration to the correlations among the stocks they hold. Over time, the average degree of diversification has improved but these improvements result primarily from changes in the correlation structure of the market. Nonetheless, improved portfolio diversification has a considerable impact on the composition and performance of investor portfolios.

A speculator should also remember that past performance is not a guarantee of future returns but it can be used as a useful indicator as to when to either buy or sell a fund. The investor needs to find out more about why performance has been good or bad and this involves asking some of the following questions:

Is the investment style out of sorts with the market that is, are they a value manager when growth is taking off?
Most people think that the key to success is analyzing the market and finding the next winner. On the contrary, the key to making is money management.

It is not our philosophy to predict and seek which investment would make money, but it is a school of thought that ensures that one can make money if the overall strategy is well managed. Our school of thought also leverages on the fact that one can have a positive expectancy by trading on the long side.

The Position Trading methodology depends on a successful investment philosophy of utilizing Diversification and Fund Switching techniques. The following section describes these investment strategies and how they correspond with different portfolios.

Sector Rotation

The goal is to constantly rotate into the best-performing funds. This method is based on the fact that distinct sectors of the economy perform differently during the same time-period. For example, in 1991, the stocks of health care companies performed well while utility companies under-performed. Yet, just a year later, in 1992, this trend reversed.

Style Rotation

The best performing funds at a given time often have a similar investment strategy. For example, when large cap growth investing is performing well, traders should rotate into large cap growth funds. Similarly, when the small cap value style of investing is providing the best results, traders should rotate into small cap value funds. This has a huge bearing on the performance of a portfolio and many investors do not understand it.

Value and growth go in and out of fashion and are often difficult to see without hindsight. Many investors in 2000 had their portfolios facing in only one direction and this caused considerable anguish when value came back. The difference lies in investing style, for example, a growth manager is primarily interested in companies with strong earnings or profits growth while a value manager looks at companies whose valuation is cheap compared with its profits, cash flow, dividends or assets.

Some of the many other investment styles include growth and value, contrarian, large-cap, small-cap, earnings momentum, asset allocation, special situations, international, global, hedging, index, sector selection, bottoms-up, tops-down, thematic, defensive, conservative, aggressive, moderate, all-weather, chameleon, high yield, hybrids, and new styles yet to be invented.

Geographic Rotation

Portions of the portfolios can be employed in this type of strategy when market conditions are favorable. When other geographic regions are providing superior results, Trend-followers may often rotate into various international funds. Special considerations must be made when investing in international funds due to additional risk and the fact that many of these funds levy redemption fees.

Example - Fund Switching

Our school of thought confines investors to think along a pragmatic and intuitive Fund Switching technique. The calculation is simple, if one has long wheat at a losing position, adding a position in soybeans is like adding to a losing position. Similarly, if there are two losing positions in one direction, even in unrelated markets, a third position in the same direction is not acceptable, as the two are already showing a loss. It is advised to drop one of the losing positions before initiating a new position. Also from a volatility view, positions in both directions will experience less volatile swings in account equity than an account with all positions in same direction.

One cannot avoid risk completely but can minimize it. The basis of successful Position Trading system is a simple n-day channel breakout entry and exit system. There are many variations on this i.e. one could risk say 1% for initial positions and 4% marked to market or 'market heat' as it's sometimes called. The idea is to limit risk and maximize profits by position-sizing and other calculations that give a reason to enter and exit the market. Here is one plan: the Kelly Criterion.

Kelly % = A - [(1-A)/B]

Where: -
A is the % of winning trades in decimal format (reliability of system) and
B is the average profitable trade in $ divided by the average losing trade in $

The reliability of a system is 0.5 and one makes twice what he risks when he wins. Thus B = 2. Therefore the amount of remaining equity he should risk to produce the maximum rate of return is

Kelly % = 0.5 - [1 - 0.5)/2] = 0.5 [0.5 / 2] = 0.5 - 0.25 = 0.25

The maximum bet then is 25%. However, our method is more straightforward and accessible. Kelly formula should be used what it is for: inspirational proof that position sizing or money management is critical to trading success.

Traders may take 80% of Kelly to be on the conservative side (20%), work out how many different markets they would be trading i.e. 10 and then allocate 2% of their trading equity per position. If the account is $100,000, then for each new position they may subtract the initial entry price from the exit price to determine "how many". Traders might be able to afford 4 wheat contracts (if the amount risked was $500 or less) only 1 Swiss Franc and may have to forgo an S&P if the initial stop was further away than $2000. If they have on 10 positions and all of them go against on one day they are still within the Kelly Criterion. This what is known as a recursive money management system, where the decision what (rather 'how many') to risk next is made AFTER a trade? This obviously requires dependency between the trades. Now for each new position, the initial entry price is subtracted from the exit price to determine "How many".

Position Traders always follow the basic cut losses short, let profits run. It is possible to profit in the long run by having initial stops to prevent the unusually large adverse moves and by a trailing stop to attempt to capture as much of the extraordinary large moves. As a result all profitable Position Trading systems have less than 50% win to loss ratios.

Trend-followers may trade a percentage of their equity on each trade - enough to do well, but not so much that they get too far. When trading like *smart money*, one might consider to increase the percentage when ahead and decrease the percentage of equity when behind.

In sum, when the down market indicator turns negative signaling "down" market conditions the recommended rules for Position Trading get modified until the market turns positive again. The basic idea is that when the market is down, get out of any even mildly down trending funds and look for one performing strongly. If there is nothing performing strongly then go to liquid markets.

The fund's composition is also a vital component in Portfolio Management and Fund Switching; Trend-followers ensure that they do not get too heavily weighted in a given sector. They should also avoid switching among similar funds.

Long trades have a high positive expectancy. When the market starts up trending (winning streak on the long side), the probability of it continuing is about 70%. Short trades have a negative expectancy and one could loose up to 20 times the amount risked. Any time if a trader risks more than 5% of equity on the short side he risks bankruptcy. The section below details portfolio adjustments during a winning/loosing streak.

How To Adjust Your Portfolio During The Winning Streak?

The key to success is being able to capture as much profit as possible from a winning trade while, at the same time, not letting the profit get away.

For example, if a winning trade went 15 days, one can make 'n' number of times the initial risk if risked the maximum continually. Invariably, if one continually risk as much as possible on a winning trade (even in off-trend), he will eventually lose all of his profits. This means that one has to raise stop at adequate time.

The long trade is one trade. A good strategy after a win is to risk 80% of the maximum on the second bet of a win streak; 70% of the maximum on the third trial; 50% of the maximum on the fourth trial; 30% of the maximum on the fifth trial and 20% thereafter. If the streak, only starts out with a one to one winner, might not want to risk more than 50% on the next trial.

Money management determines how much the risk is initially; it also controls position size during the trade. The golden rule of trading is to let the profits run by locking in some of your profits. Otherwise, a trader may loose core equity risk and all accumulated profits in that trade. Another advantage of this type of money management technique is that it is relatively easy to implement in real time. Once traders are aware of the desired pyramiding technique to use, it is easy for them to know exactly how many positions to take on the next trade, based on the results of the last trade.

Example: Once a trader has made 30%, he needs to add 15% to his capital base and apply the same strategy each 15% thereafter. Each financial year starting afresh, means after making 30%, 45%, 60%,... on each step he has put 15% of the profit in his account. This ensures a situation is prevented where a loss of 15% is a greater $ amount than a 30% loss because of a rapid escalation of capital.

Following is the explanation of the above example: the method Trend-followers use is protecting a fixed percentage of the profits earned. When the market starts up trending, one may only protect a small percentage at first, but as the trend continues, one should protect more of his profits. Followed by trail stops, by trading 80% of the maximum on day 2; 60% of the maximum on day 3; 40% on day 4; and 20% on day 5 onward.

There are a number of possible ways a trader can make use of in terms of protecting stops. For example, if 100% is risked of what is possible on days 2 and 3 of a winning streak, one might risk losing it all, but having a winner after three straight winning days.

8:1 (2^3) = (((1/0,25)^3)^0,5) = (((1/0,25)^(3*0,5))

If risked the maximum in a trade that went ten days, one would have a 512 (2^9) (((1/0,25)^9)^0,5) to one winner.

In order to get that profit, one would have to risk all of his profits on days 2 through 10 that is probably not a wise decision. Incidentally, investors can determine how much they are allowed to bet during a winning streak by risking the total equity.

How To Adjust Your Portfolio During A Losing Streak?

It can get emotionally devastating for people trading during a losing streak. The ability to properly make use of information starts to become distorted because of the impairment of the confidence factor - a by-product of a losing streak. Trend-followers work efficiently to restore that confidence, an example is by cutting back trading size and getting back into the game.

Risk control is the most important thing in trading. Adjusting the portfolio is very important during a losing streak. Traders start to reduce numbers once a predetermined level is hit. Again this is function of statistical data based on the trading history and the current volatility of the market. Trend-followers trading insist on cutting the position size down in losing trades. That way, they trade the smallest position size when the trading is worst. There is nothing better than a fresh start.

Earlier in the chapter, we discussed that trading in Liquid Market should be preferred. One may pick right spots in the bond market, because of the liquidity and way it trades, with timing he will be able to execute his trades at better prices. Also in a losing trade, he would like to get out, this where choosing a liquid market comes into picture. So one needs to pick a spot where getting out is easy. Trend-followers insist that by staying calm and getting out with resolve and continually buying it with patience can work the way out from a loosing scenario, which is evidently hard to do when one is losing money.

Trend-followers always remember that their job is to make money. In doing that they get into positions that are right. There exist numerous opportunities, but they need to recognize the trend and trade fast if they want to move in the market. Trend-followers believe in taking advantage of everything all the time.

The process of translating portfolio risk into number of units traded, under given price risk estimates, is shown here using a T-Bond position as an example.

Example 1: Proposed long position in US T-Bonds at 100

(Unit Face Value US$ 100,000)

Estimated (Accepted) Price Risk: 1.5%

Allocated Equity: US$ 5,000,000

Accepted Portfolio Risk on Position: 2%

Calculating Accepted Position Risk in absolute US$ = (5,000,000 * 2%) = 100,000

Calculating Accepted Per Unit Risk in absolute US$ = (500,000 * 1.5%) = 75,000

Accepted size of the trading position = 100,000/ 75,000= 13.3 units of T-Bonds at face value US$ 100,000 equaling a US$ 1,330,000 investment. If contract sizes do not permit the exact trade size as calculated, it is advised to round down to the lower possible trading size, here, a US$ 1,000,000 investment.

Example 2: Actual Market Price = 101

System calculates price risk to be 3% (up from 2%).

Allocated equity now at US$ 800,000 (due to losses in other markets within the portfolio)

Accepted Portfolio Risk unchanged at 1.5%

Calculating Accepted Position Risk in absolute US$ = (800,000 * 1.5%) = 12,000

Calculating Accepted Per Unit Risk in absolute US$ = (101,000 * 3%) = 3,030

Calculated accepted position size = 12,000 / 3,030 = 3.96 units of T-Bonds (at face value US$ 100,000), rounded up to 4 units, equals accepted position size of US$ 400,000. The system will therefore issue a signal to sell US$ 300,000 worth of T-Bonds in order to adjust the position to changes in the price risk and in the portfolio composition, expressed in the lower portfolio allocation.

Percentage risk and percentage return do not have a symmetric effect on the portfolio, because the required percentage return to recoup a given loss (in percent) increases geometrically with the size of the loss. Not adjusting the trading size to the portfolio value (by decreasing with greater risk) would lead to an increase of risk at an increasing rate (as expressed by the increasing leverage of a fixed-size trading position).

Conclusion

If a one makes a bad trade, but has money management then he is not much in trouble. However, if he misses a good trade there is nowhere for him to turn. Further, if a trader misses good trades with regularity then he is finished. For example, if the market is moving rapidly through a trader's buying zone and unfortunately he misses it his buy signal and instead waits for a retracement to maybe buy cheaper. But, the market just keeps going higher and higher and never retraces. Now what is he supposed to do? There's a great temptation to reason that now it's too high to buy. If he buys it now he'll have an initiation price that's too high? No, the initiation price simply won't have the kind of significance as is generally assumed after the trade is made. One cannot miss these trades. Our way of speculating will force discipline to make sure these trades are not missed.

Proper diversification of investment capital recognizes all individual investment requirements. It also recognizes the capital allocation requirement in order to obtain the maximum rate of return with the minimum relative risk.

While the well-balanced portfolio provides the most consistent returns, how you go about achieving this depends on where you are in the investment spectrum. If the client is starting off an investment portfolio and hopes to add to it over the years, then he should really start off with a mainstream fund as a core holding. If he has a fairly mature investment portfolio, it will be easier to achieve better diversification even if it means reorganizing what he has. A starting point as a model growth portfolio would therefore be for the investor to use a growth portfolio as a base and either make it more aggressive or less aggressive by the use of funds and capital allocation. The Master speculator recognizes the lack of forecasting ability and helps him to assemble a successful portfolio.

- Stocks do trend - at any point in time; there are many stocks in a trending move.
- Stocks are more volatile – dollar for dollar - a single stock moves more than a future

- Stocks don't trade inversely - there is an upward bias and other factors that make *symmetrical* systems perform poorly. You can make money with shorts but trading long and short the *same way* will not test well

- Stocks are good for smaller accounts - the amount of money required to trade a diversified portfolio of stocks is much lower than that required for futures. This is mainly because of the dollar risk implied by a single contract in futures.
- Proper selection of the Portfolio is key - there are thousands of stocks, you can't trade all the signals, you have to pick the right ones.
- Stocks move in tandem - stocks correlate very highly in terms of direction on a given day.
- Listed Stocks (NYSE) Trade Different from NASDAQ - There is a big difference in the way stocks execute and this affects their suitability for trading.

Stock based Position Trading systems the portfolio has the risk of becoming index like if too many stocks consist of the portfolio Research shows that over 20-25 different stocks are a maximum number to trade as a basket.

Speculation

Speculating as a part time business or retirement endeavor is ideal for several reasons;

1) No need for customers
2) Relatively low overhead
3) Expand by multiplying the contracts you buy

Let's look at these points in detail, shall we?

Customers what customers?

The biggest hurdle of any enterprise is to gain a basic group of followers and establish clientele. Massive advertising and giveaways are designed to do just that. Some ventures seem easy to start only to realize that your competition is massive and they can buy and sell you multiple times over. How do you compete with such a group of competitors? Well You can start by distinguishing yourself from the group and offer exceptional service. Even if you do the best job you can muster your competition will claim to be better whether it is true or not. I do not wish to elaborate on this further but we can all agree on the competitive nature of business. There is even a book called "Swim with the Sharks". A real beauty of any trading business **NEEDS NO CUSTOMERS!**

Relative low overhead

A trading business is not a huge overhead if done properly. Consider that a McDonald franchise is more than a million dollars and many other franchise and service ventures are quite expensive we can safely say – entry to trading can be done on a shoestring.
You can even trade while keep a day job. You can't do it with many other businesses since study shows that small business owner virtually work all the time.

Expansion is with push of a button

Robert Kanter the now retired president of ETG who taught me the fine art of exchange listed trading. He used to tell rookies to trade 50 shares of stocks and sometimes even less.

Once profitable he said you could expand your business by adding a zero. Consider that other businesses must go though market analysis and borrow money to expand this seems easy in comparison.

The risk of failure in trading is no different from opening a restaurant or a business venue. Statistics show that the odds are roughly equal. Upfront investments can differ of course. In trading sooner you are on the right track lower is your "tuition" to enter into the trading business. I congratulate you on buying this course and investing a little in order perhaps to save a lot more.

In addition to be a good business – futures trading can be advantageous for tax reasons as well.

I am not a tax professional so please check it with a CPA or EA but the last I heard the law was; regardless of the actual holding period, commodity profits are automatically taxed as sixty percent long-term capital gains and forty percent short-term capital gains. The current maximum capital gains rate is fifteen percent, somewhat less than the maximum rate for ordinary income.

There are other advantages of futures versus buy and hold and stock market investing. Namely one is the unbiased market direction.

As you perhaps know or heard that the stock markets have historical upward bias namely caused by inflation and other considerations (such as politics)

No such thing exists in the futures markets. The commodity markets are not upward bias and can and do go down as easy as up. Taking positions in the falling market is what futures traders call short position.

Going short in stock required the up tick rule. In addition since stocks need to be 'borrowed' to be used as shorts not all firm has equal access to this "short list" this hindered many 'bears' and forced them to trade options or use expensive strategies called 'bullets'.

There is no such problem with the futures markets. You can always go short as easy as you can go long. To clarify the terminology let me spell it out.

Shorts are betting that the market will go down.
Longs are betting that the marker will go up.

This terminology is the same in the stock markets and futures. The easy of going short pales in comparison the hardships and pain to go short in stocks – it will depend on your broker. The average retail customer has no chance to execute shorts and conventional wisdom and sometimes stupidity frowns of shorts as doomsayers and Un-American. This is the misinformation permeated from Wall Street.

Imagine a casino that has the edge in all forms of betting activity. Would this Casino tell their customers the proper ways of gaming? Well the proper ways of gaming would be **NOT PLAYING** *or* limiting yourself to the few activities that can yield profits. Card Counting and Poker are the two. No in the millions years – Casinos would ban card counting and often do not even offer poker even so they can make modest profits from it.

The situation is no different from Wall Street. Dumber the average player remains better off the inside players can do. Do not look from meaningful and informative comments from Wall Street insiders and that includes Media, Wall Street Journal.

I am not saying that there is some conspiracy or collusion out there. Simply said – much what is coming from the corner – "buy and hold is good", "mutual funds are the Holy Grail", "futures are inherently more dangerous than stocks" are all nonsense yet they were all invented and permeated to confuse and keep the average folk in the dark.

Real life shows that "buy and hold" can put you in the poorhouse, Mutual fund can rip off and overcharge the public, and stock trading can lose the greenback the same way as futures trading. The latest buzz is day trading. It is a great money machine to clearing firms, Big Clearing Firms and their LLP partners.

Yes, you can make money in day trading and by all means try it if that is what you want. But watch out for anything that is promoted and pushed too much in the mainstream. It is often done with a false pretense.

Do not let this stop you from following your dreams. Trade the ways your heart desires and follow your dream but do it with one foot at least on earn firmly grounded while you reach for the sky.

Practically everything that's been written during the past fifty years has been a restatement of Wyckoff, Livermore. One of the most important lessons I learned from all three was to trade what you see, not what you think. This course however has been updated to the 21st century and offers my 20-years of experience coupled with an excellent teaching tool, Track N' Trade Pro.

Liquidation Rules

Liquidations are more significant than initiations!

It is not likely Smart Money to consider initiating positions at random, but it is good liquidation strategy that promises profits. *Smart Money* was also taught that they should capture 55-65% of the major trend, not 10-15%. This gives liquidation criteria all the more significance in our system.

As we know that the rule number one of this system is to be prepared to accept losses. Experienced traders do not let losses hurt their consciousness. They trade in a manner that liquidation strategy helps them to achieve their goal. Hence, stops whether mental or actual are essential.

Conclusively, a stop must be used in view of preserving the capital.

Stops

Stops are the perfect method to control risk. A stop is mechanical in nature; it will turn on by itself when the time comes – best suited to trader who can't pull the trigger. When trading like Smart Money, the stops are categorized into two types. The first limits a percentage of the total trade and the second limits the trade in view of certain time frame.

What is the Basic Rule for Stops? They must be balanced from a time point of view (4 week low, etc.) and the money management scheme (two ATR against). Read on for details.

Stop Rules

For the entry, *Smart Money* uses a 1/2 ATR protective stop. If Smart Money finds that on day of entry the market goes 1/2% against on initiation day, they would get out of that position immediately. Tight stops are best for initiation positions. This is followed by a 2% hard stop and a 2 ATR stop. Larger the stops, longer are the trades and greater are the profits with a looser stop. Unlike loosing trades, winning trades should not be kept on a tight leash. A 6 ATR retreating to 5 1/2 ATR has less expectation loss than 1 ATR retracing to 1/2 ATR.

In the following section we will understand the stop rules by getting back to the system process.

We know that the system builds up profitable positions by 1/2 ATR increases. In other words, when the position has 1/2 ATR gain, it allows addition of one unit. Lets understand how to place stops in such a situation with an example.
$500/unit is the price, 1 ATR is $6. The trader owns 10 units at the end. Buying the first unit at $500, the original stop is placed at $488, since the 2 ATR stop is valued at $12. Adding at 1/2 ATR increments, the second unit will be added at $503. At this point, Smart Money moves the stop from the first unit (at $488 to $490).
This gradual move of stops is very important. At this time, we have two units, and both have stops at $488. The process is repeated for the first five units.
Always remember that the stops must never be moved beyond initiation price. By doing this, the stops cushions down drift in price and strengthens the building of a position.
For example, if a trader is at 1500 that started with 1000, it is a 50% gain. We in such a scenario will never let the whole 50% gain go off the table because there will be other

liquidation criteria that would have taken place. I.e. see rule "a certain number of weeks against."

Time of Trade	Loss Situation
Initiation Point	2 ATR (automatic stop point) Loss
5 ATR Profit	7 ATR (unlikely to occur) Loss
9 ATR Profit (Liquidation signals will appear)	11 ATR (unlikely to occur) Loss (Liquidation signals will appear)

Figure 2

Stops should never be moved past breakeven levels. Initiating the 5th unit within the pyramiding scheme, all subsequent stops must be placed at breakeven. At the same time Smart Money must be willing to loose. While doing so, they will be protecting larger profits regardless of the order when positions were taken. Further more, Smart Money would want to place a stop moving up in the direction of the trend as profits accumulate.

Another important aspect of Position Trading system is that it considers all positions independent of each other for the purpose of determining stops, units, etc. Consequently, Smart Money does not average the positions. They keep things rigidly systematic and organized. Is it getting easier?

Absolute Liquidation

Absolute Liquidation is when ATR stop is set off especially at initiation, the account does not have sufficient equity to avail another trade, liquidating largest loss or smallest gain, and 10 or 20 days is against position.

As with entry, Smart Money scale in, and on exits they scale-out. When the position is suffering a number of days against it, Smart Money does not wait for the pre-set rule: 20 days against the position to liquidate the whole position. Instead, they liquidate 1/3 of position at 10 days against, 1/3 at 15 days against, and the final 1/3 at 20 days against.

Additionally, regardless of profit or loss if volatility doubles from the time of initiation, Smart Money considers it good to get out. This doesn't let volatility whipsaw their position. Whipsaw is when instead of taking a 2% risk on each trade, the stops are placed at 1/2 ATR for 1/2% account risk. If a Unit has been stopped out, it would be re-entered if the market reached the original entry price.

The Whipsaw also had the added benefit of not requiring the movement of stops for earlier Units as new Units were added, since the total risk would never exceed 2% at the maximum four Units. The basic concept of liquidation has been given below:

When the liquidation is at 2, 3, 4 week intervals
Instead of waiting for 4 weeks against, Smart Money should liquidate 1/3 at 2 weeks against, 1/3 at 3 weeks against and finally the last third at 4 weeks against.

Double ATR liquidations

Whether it is a Profit or a loss, if the volatility doubles from initiation point exit trade, then Smart Money considers it wise to get out of that position.
Smart Money trade at the breakout when it exceeds during the day, and do not wait until the daily close or the open of the following day.

In the case of opening gaps, we enter positions on the open if a market open through the price of the breakout.

Basic Breakout Strategy

To exit a profitable position, the entry, money management and other factors are taken into consideration altogether. Smart Money enters on breakouts and most breakouts do not result in trends. If the winning trades do not earn enough on average to offset these losses, they may loose money.

There are many different ways to identify when the market has made a break out. The general rule is that the price bar must close on a new high or low.

False breakouts do exist. False breakouts can be very annoying as well as misleading. Using following tools can alleviate problems and frustrations associated with a high or low tick due to stop loss activity:

- The Average Directional Index that determines whether a market is trending or not; it has nothing to do with direction,
- The ADX line that is found hidden away within the indicator called Directional Movement Indicator (provides the direction as it displays the ADX line).

Using n and n1 period Moving Averages (MAV) provides the directional signal when they cross. A cross of the n period MAV from below and up through the n1 period MAV means that prices are advancing or moving higher at a faster rate than they have been.

When the ADX moves up two days or bars, the MAV's have crossed to give a buy signal. A buy signal; so traders buy on the open of the next bar and place your initial stop half way between the ranges that the market had just broken out from.

The opposite is correct for a sell signal. As the market moves in favor, trail the stop up using your own money management techniques to lock in profit.

Liquidation During A Winning Streak

The key to success in the Trend Trading is be able to capture as much profit as possible from a winning trade while, at the same time, not letting the profit get away.

If a winning trade went 15 days, one can make 'n' number of times the initial risk if risked the maximum continually. Invariably, if one continually risks as much as possible on a winning trade (even in off-trend), he will eventually lose all of his profits. This means that one has to RAISE STOP AT ADEQUATE TIME.

The long trade is one trade. A good strategy after a win is to risk 80% of the maximum on the second bet of a win streak; 70% of the maximum on the third trial; 50% of the maximum on the fourth trial; 30 % of the maximum on the fifth trial and 20% thereafter. If the streak, only starts out with a one to one winner, one may not want to risk more than 50% on the next trial.

There are a number of possible ways a trader can make use of in terms of protecting stops. For example, if 100% is risked of what is possible on days 2 and 3 of a winning streak, one might risk losing it all, but having a winner after three straight winning days.

8:1 (2^3) = (((1/0,25)^3)^0,5) = (((1/0,25)^(3*0,5))

If risked the maximum in a trade that went ten days, one would have a 512 (2^9) (((1/0,25)^9)^0,5) to one winner.

In order to get that profit, one would have to risk all of his profits on days 2 through 10 that is probably not a wise decision.

Liquidation During A Losing Streak

Liquidation is very important during a losing streak. Traders start to reduce numbers once a predetermined level is hit. Again this is a function of statistical data based on the trading history and the current volatility of the market. Smart Money insists on cutting the position size down in losing trades. That way, they trade the smallest position size when the trading is worst.

We have discussed that trading in Liquid Market should be preferred. One may pick right spots in the bond market, because of the liquidity and way it trades, with timing he will be able to execute his trades at better prices. Also in a losing trade, traders would like to get out of that position; this is where liquid market comes into picture. So one needs to pick a spot where getting out is easy.

The process of translating portfolio risk into number of units traded, under given price risk estimates, is shown here using a Crude Oil position as an example.

Actual Market Price = 101
System calculates price risk to be 3% (up from 2%).
Allocated equity now at US$ 800,000 (due to losses in other markets within the portfolio)
Accepted Portfolio Risk unchanged at 1.5%
Calculating Accepted Position Risk in absolute US$ = (800,000 * 1.5%) = 12,000
Calculating Accepted Per Unit Risk in absolute US$ = (101,000 * 3%) = 3,030

Calculated accepted position size = 12,000 / 3,030 = 3.96 units of Crude Oil (at face value US$ 100,000), rounded up to 4 units, equals accepted position size of US$ 400,000. The system will therefore issue a signal to sell US$ 300,000 worth of Crude Oil in order to adjust the position to changes in the price risk and to make maximum out of liquidation rules.

Percentage risk and percentage return do not have a symmetric effect on the portfolio, because the required percentage return to recover a given loss (in percent) increases geometrically with the size of the loss. Avoiding liquidation would lead to an increase of risk at an increasing rate (as expressed by the increasing leverage of a fixed-size trading position).

Conclusion

Our rules don't favor liquidation. Position liquidations are activated by significant unfavorable price action and are never pre-determined objectives. There is just one simple rule for traders: concentrate on managing the risk and the returns will take care of themselves.

From the above discussion it is clear that *smart money* liquidates unprofitable positions early. They believe that a position must return a profit and if it does not, and especially if it is going against their current position, they should get out. To do that, they use actual stop orders or mental stop orders. They believe that they should always use stop orders. Also, if some of the positions traded are big losers, means that the trader didn't cut losses quickly enough or has been spreading equity across too many positions. Liquidation is suggested in most of the cases.

Liquidation requires great discipline to watch your profits evaporate in order to hold onto your positions for the really big move. The ability to maintain discipline and stick to the rules during large winning trades is the hallmark of the experienced successful trader.

Always try to learn from your mistakes. After you complete each trade, write a detailed analysis, explaining what did and did not work.

Modern Portfolio Theory

Fixed income and dividend plays should be a part of everyone's portfolio. The only question is the portfolio allocation method and accumulation. The level of bullishness in regards of the stock market is in the eye of the beholder. There is no reason to dwell upon this. Even if the US stock market should remain in a sideways pattern one should invest some money in fixed income assets. This is according to Modern Portfolio Theory.

The rationale behind this is again comes back to risk management. Fixed income is usually safer and more reliable than volatile commodities and futures markets.

Modern Portfolio Theory is the geometrical opposite to the traditional Sock picking idea that permeates the bookstores and modern investment literature.

Time Horizon

Time horizon from investing to actually retirement should be the paramount factor in the decision making process of the Speculator.

Retirement for certain people may involve more active type retirement where certain activities still take up the time of the person but the Corporate "rat race" and other stress inducing activities are eliminated. Typically this time is at age 65 when the person can get Medicare so Health insurance will not a problem for them. Other people who have military or police background would get their Health coverage via the Veteran's Administration or other agencies earlier so their time horizon will change accordingly.

Once the Speculator determined the approximate time horizon he/she can start a plan. The basic idea is longer time one has until retirement less importance should be placed on fixed income and Preferred Stocks and more risk can be taken in other areas like stocks, Exchange Traded Funds for foreign issues, sector funds and of course my favorite, Commodities.

Even if the person is a model investor and starts planning at age 21, which is rare - he/she should invest *all asset allocation classes* at the same time. This means buying a house should be the priority buy some retirement plan such as an IRA, 401K should also be started as soon as possible. Ten dollars a week or more is enough. One does not need to start with a lot of money. The *power of compounding* and time will take care of the rest.

The important matter is that if one cherishes ones family (or future family) and wish to live happily and securely long into his/hers golden age – one must *act*.

A disciplined approach will yield result, procrastination and poor spending habits will defeat the best laid out plan.

If the reader is doubtful of the seriousness of this matter just consider the current trends and policy shifts in Washington. It is doubtful that Corporations and/or the Government will want to bail out the undisciplined and spend happy citizen.

A good way to change ones ways is to absolutely limit and curtail ones use of credit cards.

Financial Planners

Should you use a financial planner? It is the opinion of the author that the individual is the best planner of his or hers destiny. Most financial planners will not offer secrets; their approach is no more than common sense and ideas that can be found in myriads of books such as mine.

There is also a consideration how would a Financial Planner make any money from his or hers efforts. Is it via Commission or a fixed charge? If the reader is absolutely vehement in using a planner the fixed charge planner should be preferred.

Most common approach of the financial services industry lately is a percentage of managed money.

Usually the people who use such services are the well-healed businesspersons who have assets in six figures or more. Average people usually do not get phone solicitation from Merrill Lynch.

A good way to do research for investment ideas using newfound knowledge of risk management is the Internet.

Scalping Exchange Traded Funds

When this author traded stocks in the early 1990's there were no Day trading firms proliferating the Speculative landscape.

It was possible to speculate New York Stock Exchange listed issues with relative ease if one

Had access to execution and professional level commission fees.

One relatively easy methodology was to *Scalp*, which is quickly to trade in and out of larger positions of Municipal Bond or Preferred Stock Exchange Traded funds.
These funds have a rather decent yield that is paid monthly and in addition the bid and ask spread is usually large enough to make money with these are virtually no risk.
Traders who specialized in these issues made in access of fifty thousand dollars a month depending of the level of trading capital they had access to via trading firms.
In addition to profits made by *scalping* these funds paid 7-10 percent interest annually that was paid and distributed monthly in form of dividends.

Decimalization

The change over began in August 2000, when the NYSE began trading seven stocks in decimals. The number was expanded to 57 companies in September. By February 2001, the stock in all the 3,025 companies listed on the NYSE - about 280.9 billion shares – had completed the transition and Specialist trading started in decimals, or pennies.

Most people have abandoned Scalping as a technique when decimalization hit the New York Stock Exchange. Interestingly despite decimalization certain ETFs that are not traded in excess of 100,000 shares per day, still have a bid/ask spread of 20-25 cents.

Psychology

"Men who can both be right and sit tight are uncommon. I found it one of the hardest things to learn. But it is only after a stock operator has firmly grasped this that he can make big money. It is literally true that millions come easier to a trader after he knows how to trade than hundreds did in the days of his ignorance."

Jesse Livermore

Wealth is the product of man's capacity to think. Money rests on the axiom that every man is the owner of his mind and his effort. Money demands that a trader sells, not his weakness, but his talent and his reasoning. It also demands that a trader buys, not any available shoddiest offer, but the best that money can find.

It is understood that when men start living on trade, their final arbiter is reasoning and not force. The degree of a man's productiveness is: his wins and his performance through the best judgment and highest ability. So it cannot be rued out that this is the code of existence where the bait is money.

We are conditioned to avoid risk, isn't this the first thing that is taught to us in an early age. To be safe in all conditions is the advice we receive and even pass on. From a conventional point of view: we consider risk to have only bad side. Few people have thought unconventionally on taking risks and the most prominent of these people are the day traders and the gamblers. It has come to their realization that the conventional view of risk is shortsighted and often mistaken.

Unconventional mostly successful people understand that when risk is handled properly, it may be highly productive. These people, through years, have debated the fact that risk is an advantage to be used rather than a pitfall to be avoided. Calculated risks, as they say, is quite different from being rash.

Much could be associated with Psychology of trading and the factors responsible for success in trading. We will first understand these factors as the reasons that lure the traders and gamblers to be active in the market. Furthermore, we will understand the motivating factors that would throw some light on why people day-trade and gamble. And at the end of this section we will understand the pitfalls that should be avoided in trading – this is something professionals have mastered, the smooth running with a touch of experience compels people to get back to the market.

Psychology Of Trading And The Factors Responsible For Success In Trading

A person who understands how to react under stress is the best trader. It may seem to be a plain sentence, but it holds the essence of winning in speculating.

The reasons? When under stress people with different personalities behave in different ways. Self-awareness and some basic techniques to offset sub-optimal behavior go a long way. Few of these self-awareness techniques are listed on the next page. Let us understand this with the help of an example, when investors believe that markets repeat movements, they look for patterns. With the help of numerous tools they take market data and form various patterns mechanically, statistically or mathematically. Choosing to repeat both experiences and their responses, these people aim to make their life comfortable by having familiar things around them.

On the other hand, people who are confident about themselves and their strategies make the most. No matter how good a person is at analyzing the market, if he does not have confidence, all what he is really doing is repeatedly creating situations that might respond with extreme frustration. So the confidence that a person has accumulated over the years is always at test, people do enjoy high adrenal rush.

Confidence comes through knowledge and by practicing discipline over years of trading. The knowledge combined with the use of what one has learned makes a successful trader. The more successful a trader is, the less fearful he becomes and more he wants to play. And this how your confidence will grow.

Taking risks and winning depends significantly on the trading styles. The non self-employed gamblers showed a preference for jobs, which allow them to be "out on the road" and away from supervision.

Another trait that is linked to trading markets is pervasive irrational exuberance. Surely, Overconfidence and Magical Thinking are few unavoidable human tendencies. A professional knows best to avoid these loopholes. Lets have a look at these tendencies and its affect on trading and how successful speculators handle these:

Overconfidence

It has been noticed that thinking that they know more than they do, people express their opinion as fact on subjects they actually know little about. Instead of listening, they talk and instead of waiting patiently, they act speculatively. This is something one should always avoid. Instead of reacting to market rumors, Trend-followers act with skepticism.

Magical Thinking

Magical thinking is the role of intuition and subjective speculation about how markets will act. By assessing innermost thoughts about money and self worth, people label these patterns of thought as magical thinking. Habitual speculator constitutes of a large share in market volume, yet the profile and motivation of these people are not well understood. On the one hand, the traditional regulatory literature views these traders as ill prepared, unsophisticated, unaware of the risks, and undercapitalized; such a profile is used to justify calls for strict regulation. On the other hand, most economic theory models the speculator's behavior as rational, i.e., they are assumed to be risk averse, profit-motivated investors. There is no magical thinking concept involved in Prudent Speculating. Logical reasoning supports every move in this school of thought.

Motivating Factors

People may find no relationship between the specific recreational motivational item and trading but studies have proved recreational utility to be the primary trading stimulus. Psychologists who studied habitual gamblers supported the recreational consumption in the market. Referring to gamblers in general, three categories were defined:

- Profit motivated
- Compulsive
- Leisure consumers
- Vast majority falls into the "leisure consumption" category.

The enjoyment of betting or risk taking and the sense of being important in the action are more important to them than winning or losing money.

It is said that gamblers who are highly energetic, extremely competitive, and aggressive, extrovert, and hard working have great inclination toward commission and fee-based employment such as insurance sales, stock brokerage, mobile home sales, and law. What is the basis of this observation? How can we find out what motivates a trader?

Motivation factors can be known by assessing the relationship between:

Independent variables such as age, educational level, income, net worth, years of trading experience, and frequency of trading, and the

Dependent variable, "number of contracts a speculator holds open at one time."

It has been proved that these variables were directly related to day- trading and gambling. The results indicated that the traders with high trade frequencies trade the largest number of contracts on average.

Income significantly related to trading quantity. More the income more is the frequency of trading.

The average age of speculators may reflect that significant wealth is required to speculate; people aging 55 and more generally have accumulated more capital than younger segments of the population.

Studies were also conducted to assess the relationship between:

Independent variables age, educational level, income, net worth, years of trading experience, and frequency of trading, and

Dependent variable "client's total account history gain/loss record.

The findings were that "as the frequency of trading" increases the "client's account history net gain/loss figure" decreases. Numerous studies have shown that long term position trading tends to be more profitable than short term "in and out" trading. Past studies have also shown that transaction costs contribute significantly to net account losses.

Behavioral finance research helps to develop a clearer understanding of the psychological traps investors fall in. Through years of experience, professionals are aware of these traps and are best positioned to avoid these traps. They know the form a trap could take and which one is most likely to fall into.

Five Common Pitfalls

Being Overconfident

As discussed earlier, people consistently overrate their abilities, knowledge, and skill — mostly in areas outside of their expertise. A good investor is one who seeks and weighs quality feedback and stays within his circle of competence.

Not being Vigilant

While making a decision, people often give uneven weight to the first information that they receive. Seeking information from a variety of sources and viewing various perspectives may avoid risk.

Improper Framing

Presentation of a problem may also affect a decision. Same problems framed in varied ways can cause people to make different choices. This is an important factor that assesses probabilities.

Irrational Decisions

Traders are comfortable making choices that justify past decisions, even in changed circumstances. They should instead consider only future costs and benefits.

Confirmation Trap

Investors have the tendency to seek information to support their existing point of view, but they forget that by doing this they avoid information that contradicts their opinion.

Concept

It is understood that no one can predict market consistently over the long term. It is also accepted that, to get rich, traders need to be in the market for long term. Considering these factors we cannot rule out that a trend may exist in the market. Position Trading assumes markets have trends, in such a case traders only need to identify it and then buy or sell at right time.

Another important aspect our Position Trading school of thought is that it never predicts price: never forecast trends and never act on hunches, intuition or tips. In other words, *smart money* does not anticipate markets, but react to them.

Position Trading

None would disagree to the fact that the foundation for success in speculating in any market lays in using professional money management strategies. The initiation signal for taking a position, which is either the 20-day break out, and the 55-day breakout is secondary to the thought process after the trade has been made.

Most traders fail not at the time of entering a position but after. Most crucial decisions one can make relate to the whole portfolio of ones holding and position management of existing trades.

Yet interestingly most trading systems are focusing on entry timing and almost obsessed with getting better than fifty percent win rate. This approach is not statistically sound.

I do not doubt that some short-term systems can have a better than 50 percent win rate if they are heavily optimized to a certain market. Long-term testing and real money trading often proves these systems less than robust.

The successful speculator is who practices sound money control. This is the reason why even before entering a trade, the first thing to decide is how much a person is risking. The basic reason behind this is that money management is an important deciding factor that helps a trader to know how many shares or contracts to trade. The number of contracts to trade is a crucial decision as it determines both risk and profit. There is just one thing that a trader should remember always: while he is here to make money, he won't make any if he goes broke. So the key here is not to go broke. This can be achieved by taking small positions that prevent blowouts.

Another thing that should be always kept in mind is that when trading one only plays the odds. Even if a trader trades on a setup that is correct 75% of the time, he should not forget that each trade is a random event. Trading doesn't take into account the last trade; as a result, a system that is correct 75% of the times can go wrong 25% may be ten times in a row. There is much similarity between trading and flipping coins where each flip is independent of the last. The chance of heads or tails occurring on a roll is a random occurrence and that is the reason why one can roll 100 heads in a row. Similarly, certain percentage of trades works out and a certain percentage does not. Conclusively, even if a person has the world's most accurate method, over time he will go broke if he doesn't practice good money management and risk control. This is the reason why it is said that the foundation for success in trading in any market lays in using professional money management strategies.

"Managing Money And Controlling Risks" has been the weakness of most of the traders. Studies suggest that 2% risk on any one trade makes trading conditions most favorable for a trader. The researchers suggested not more than 2% risk based on the fact that: if one is not going to get rich then he is also not going bankrupt. Researchers also believed that this strategy has low risk that enables trader to freely. In other words, if a trader risks small amount, he will not have much at stake. This will save him from a position where a bad trade has turned into a terrible investment.

If people think that trading is an easy game, they are wrong. In trading even the most experienced traders need support to make more profitable decisions. To understand Money Management in trading it is very important to first understand trader's 'chief enemies'. These enemies are inseparable from human nature to hope and to fear. People fear that a loss may develop into a bigger loss, and hope that profit may become a bigger profit. These factors keep the trader from making serious money. More of these factors are discussed in the sections to come.

Money Management

Position Trading

Position Trading works because human beings are psychologically ill equipped to profitably interact with the markets. Speculators realize that when money is involved, psychological factors interfere with the ability to reason and decide. As a result, people take their losses too late and their profits too soon.

As we know that the most successful types of Position Trading systems are based on cutting losses and letting profits run.

Prudent speculating is based on the Position Trading systems. Position Trading systems work because returns distribution for most products, especially futures, do not follow the bell curve

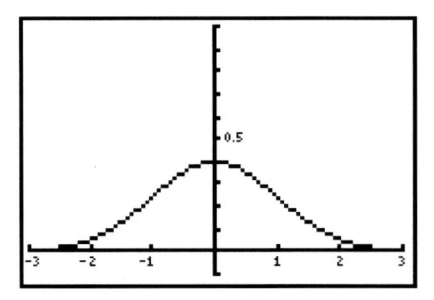

Figure 3

(Gaussian distribution). The distributions instead are based on large moves (leptokurtotic). The "D-mark effect," as shown above is not the case for the D-mark's five-day distributions. The number of cases here are 2.4 times beyond three standard deviations that would happen with a normal distribution (68% of the data within one standard deviation of the mean, 95% within two standard deviations and 99.5% within three standard deviations). The distribution that has higher peaks at the mean and fat tails has the tendency to trend, may be in cycles.

Quite different from Leptokurtotic - Gaussian distribution, they have an infinite or undefined variance - the average deviation of the data set from its mean – calculated by:

$V = 1/N$ summation of $(D_i - M)^2$

Where

$i = 1$ to N

Where N is the number of elements,

M is the same mean and

D is the current value.

Standard deviation = the square root of the variance.

For an undefined variance when the standard deviation increases on a data set the number of data points increases too. For a defined variance, it would reach a given level and then stabilize.

Market Wizards consider that the key in trading a Position Trading system is to realize that win is likely 25% to 45% of all trades and with drawdowns of around 30%. Narrowing it down to a brief conclusion: understanding these statistics and trading a basket of commodities, one can make profit in the long run.

And if we could identify false breakouts and the strength of a trend early enough, we could dramatically increase the performance of a Position Trading approach. This has been discussed in details in the technical analysis unit of this book.

Money Management

As discussed earlier the most crucial concern for a trader is how many contracts to trade. Apart from some personal psychological issues money management in successful speculating determines "how many" or "how much?" How many units of investment should be put at a given time? How much risk should be taken? It is very important for a trader to understand this concept as the question "how much" that determines the risk involved, the profit potential, whether a trader has enough new money to trade additional positions considering the risk and reward ratio.

Let us see what world's top traders and investors have to say about the importance of money management.

"Risk management is the most important thing to be well understood. Under trade, under trade, under trade is my second piece of advice. Whatever you think your position ought to be, cut it at least in half." - Bruce Kovner

"Never risk more than 1% of your total equity in any one trade. By risking 1%, I am indifferent to any individual trade. Keeping your risk small and constant is absolutely critical." - Larry Hite

"You have to minimize your losses and try to preserve capital for those very few instances where you can make a lot in a very short period of time. What you can=t afford to do is throw away your capital on sub-optimal trades." - Richard Dennis

"Risk management is the most important thing to be well understood. Under trade, under trade, under trade is my second piece of advice. Whatever you think your position ought to be cut it at least in half" - Bruce Kovner

Starting on with understanding Money Management with Position Trading, it first requires a trader to diversify his portfolio into a number of different investments or products. If a single contract/share involving money management strategies is tested, even the best trading approach may turn out not to be the best approach. So it is better to diversify to get the best results.

Diversification in speculating exposes the portfolio over the various trades or investments giving each one an equal chance of making money. Simply said, money management is a concept that keeps a trader in the game to play another day.

Secondly, money management is not inseparable from Risk Management. Risk management in trading, as we know, is the difference between success and failure.

Thirdly, money management is not Stop Placement, as it does not address the "how much" question. Managing money by having a "money management stop" means getting out of a position where a predetermined amount of money has been lost. These stops do not determine "how much" or "how many", so it has nothing to do with Money Management.

Successful traders consider trading correctly to be 90% Money Management, yet this is something most people don't understand.

So what role does money management play? In the following sections of this unit and in the chapters to follow, the issues given below will be addressed to understand the vitality of Money Management strategies in our system:

- How to handle capital preservation vs. how to handle capital appreciation

- When is it appropriate to expect success

- Capital allocation in each trade

- How much loss could be taken to avoid larger losses and when

- Strategies to follow while trading in a losing streak

- Things to keep in mind while trading in both long and short positions

- How does commodities affect trading

- How to handle correlation in trading

- Adjustments that are necessary for new accumulated profits

- Handling stops in a volatility market

- Methods to limit entry risk with options

- Preparations for unforeseen big trends

- Psychological preparations if money must be viewed as a means of keeping score.

The Reader MUST understand: when using our system, win/loss ratio, percent winning trades, etc. are of little value to decision-making. So what all are the strategies that should be used for perfect results?

There are numerous money management strategies that can be used. In this unit we will understand different money management strategies that work.

Now we know thoroughly that money management rules dictate the number of contracts or shares, but how are these decisions taken. We will understand this in-depth but first let us first understand what exactly is a money management decision: a money management decision might be that a person does not have enough money to put on any positions because the risk is too big. Determination of the number of units in each trade in a portfolio allows a trader to determine the reward and risk characteristics.

There are precise formulas involved in this concept that set the trade size. People using a constant trading size give up the edge as a blackjack player does. In both the cases the betting size is the same regardless of what cards are on the table or what the market conditions are.

Illustrated below are systems that show money management strategies at work. Professional gamblers often play low expectancy games. They master their trades just by acting by the realization that money management is the key to success. Prudent speculators follow the same system.

Gamblers consider following two money management strategies -

- Martingale System

- Anti-martingale System

Martingale system increases winnings during a losing streak. The concept has been explained by following example: while playing red and black at the roulette wheel, a gambler is paid a dollar for every dollar he risks. His odds of winning are less than 50% on each trial. The system based on money management follows the assumption that after a few losses, win eventually is assured. As a result and as per this system the gambler starts with one bet - one dollar and doubles the bet after every loss. Eventually when he would win, he will make a dollar from the entire sequence. The logic is clear. It was sure that he would win eventually.

This money management strategy is good with none but one disadvantage. The long losing streaks can prove to be a great trouble. When the odds are less than 50% in favor, one may have a streak of ten losses in a row in a 1,000 trials. By the time he reaches ten in a row, $3,050 is what he would be betting in order to come out a dollar ahead. This means that his reward-to-risk ratio is 1 to 3050. As a result, martingale-betting systems, where the risk is more when one is losing, just do not work.

Anti-martingale systems, where a gambler increases risk as he wins, often do work. When on a winning streak smart gamblers know how to increase their bets. This face of money management system directs the trader to increase the risk size when winning.

Money Management in prudent speculating involves profitable technical and profitable fundamental trading. These are dependent on inefficient markets, as efficient markets would anyway prevent any system from making profits from the markets.

Technical trading is a dependable concept because it correctly assumes that few market fundamentals remain unknown until the profit opportunity has passed. For example, fundamental analysis that excluded the possibility of an American invasion of Iraq in 2003 is incomplete and possibly unprofitable. This was the only fundamental that was worth knowing, yet remained unknown until the first strike.

Technical analysis gives advance warning about position that could be taken. Often when the true major fundamentals are unknown one can lose money being in the market at wrong time. Smart traders accept that the markets reflect reality and make reactive moves.

What is Smart Trading? Lets first try and answer what not is Smart Trading:

Preoccupation with 12 month returns is not smart trading and
Focusing on quarterly reporting

Smart trading is having adequate capital to survive drawdowns. Smart trading involves the proper use of protective stops, profit targets and allocation of capital. In smart trading risks taken should be based on the current volatility of the market, as it lets the market to show them a predefined percentage of new equity before they can add on more units. We will understand this in detail in view of Position Trading later in this chapter.

Optimizing Capital Usage - Position-sizing And its Effects

With the growing trading and investing industry, more and more companies have started focusing on education of traders. These companies promise greater wealth and market success, but only a few of the methods have been verified empirically. "Money Management" or "Asset Allocation" or "Position-Sizing", have proven scientific support. This is what we will discuss in this section of the unit.

Market Wizards have emphasized the importance of money management in stock and futures trading, *smart money* defines money management as "how much of available capital is to be allocated in a specific market position", also called Position Size. Trend-followers consider asset allocation more important than stock selection or timing. It has been established that asset allocation holds primary importance, accounting for 91.5% of the differential return of the pension funds.

Our system desires the traders to have the ability to view their portfolios as a whole. This is important because sometimes decisions are based on a defensive or reactive view of risk, in which they measure risk to avoid losses, to an offensive or proactive posture in which risks are actively managed for a more efficient use of capital. Risk can only be managed if the portfolio is viewed as a whole. The Position Trading risk management formulas and philosophies are key to increasing profits while controlling risk. We will understand this in detail later in this book.

To understand position sizing, it is important to first understand where the market is going. Please refer "Position Sizing" in the beginning of this chapter for details. From these details we know that several big trends in a year are key to success. Smart Money usually speculates for the outsized large move, where the strategy is to cut losing positions quickly.

When trading like Trend-followers it is not important to understand the trading market, it just requires the trader to take the price data and apply the rules. All markets, in a Position Trading system, are the same because of price. A speculator only makes decisions based on the facts (price) in the market. Their individual price movements most directly measure all markets. Trend-followers do not predict nor forecast. They do not jump to conclusions based on what they think they know. The trading for them derives from what the market offers, not from their own forecast. It should always be remembered that this system is not optimized to particular markets or market conditions.

Entry and Exit is not a crucial issue in trading. Consider a hypothetical situation where a trader has an entry that wins 80% of the time but wins very little money for him. Another situation can be where a trader loses 20% of the time, but when he loses, his losses far exceed his wins the other 80% of the time. Think about it. Good traders buy higher and sell lower all along, focusing on how much money they are making or losing. Buying higher means that they buy more as a trend moves up and as the price increases. For example, looking back into the past, traders know a market went from 5 to 100. Now the question is when to buy? Is it at price levels of 5, 6 or 7 or at 20 or 30? Prudent Speculating recommends traders to buy more as the trend progresses. Trying to buy low is not advisable as by that time it is not sure whether it would go to 100. Buying at 20 or 30 ensures that the trader is fully prepared with a precise well thought out strategy.

It should be remembered that identifying a potential trend is maybe 10% of the overall success of a long-term trading system. The key is not where one enters and whether one has a profit or loss on a position. The key is how big should you be trading based on market volatility.

The level of the market is not significant; the only thing significant is the market's volatility. For example, if it's the day of a crash or the day after a crash, the volatility is a lot bigger. Trading smaller is recommended in such case. The concept that where a trader enters is not critical; relevant is his current position, his equity and where the market is now.

There is no stated minimum capital to trading as the *Smart Money*. Starting capital should depend on the trader's personal discipline and his ability to stick with a system. The strategy is: rather than focusing on starting capital, one should decide how he would trade, as a wide variety of instruments is available for him to trade. Wide variety of instruments may include, stocks, currencies, and commodities across exchanges in nearly every major city in the world.

Currency markets allow traders to use up to 50:1 leverage. A person can execute trades up to $100,000 with an initial margin of $2000. However, while leverage allows traders to maximize their profit potential, potential for loss is also not less. A more conservative margin trade would be 5:1 or 10:1, but ultimately it is based on your tolerance for risk.

Trading commodities may involve high leverage, giving high profit potential and risk potential. A $1,350 security deposit will control a Silver futures contract, which contains 5,000 ounces of silver. So when the price of Silver is at $5/oz. the contract is valued at $25,000. A change in the price of Silver by 1 cent results in a $50 change in the value of futures contract either for or against the trader. A Silver price move of 10 cents in favor will make $500 in profit.

When trading in a simulated stock market, using a trading system with expected value of < 1.0, one should take positions in sizes of approximately 3.7% - 6.6% as the surviving traders, rather than 22.9% - 23.7% as the bankrupt traders.

If the traders trade over the long run, there is a greater chance of getting opportunities of great returns, than standing by the sidelines. The first part of Larry Hite's basic rules about winning in trading is given below:

- If you don't bet, you can't win.
- If you lose all your chips, you can't bet."

If a trader bets big he will lose big when he loses. Similarly, if he bets big he would win big when the draw goes his way.

It has also been noticed that risk seeking seems to diminish with experience. The active traders perform better than the traders with little or no experience. The willingness to take risks is highly dependent of what is at stake.

In order to minimize the risk of anyone tampering with the data forms, future studies are encouraged to gather the data electronically, by using computer-generated versions of data forms. Finally, decreasing the risk of getting ruined is highly inspiring (refer the risk control section for details).

If a trader has a long position, then prices need to rise before he/she is gaining any profit. If the trader is short, then prices must decline to make him/her a profit. The market moves regardless of the position of one particular trader. In order to make money trading, one must be positioned on the right side when prices are moving.

When the market moves against the trader's position and he decides it is time to close the trade, the price movement multiplied by position size determines the size of the loss. Accordingly, the risk can be estimated as the drop from entry point to exit point, that is, the difference between actual buying price and predetermined selling price multiplied by the number of shares sold. Following this reasoning, the potential profit that one can receive depends on price rise and position size.

So the emphasis should be directed toward maximizing gains, two concepts of position-sizing strategies are "letting the profits run" and "cutting losses short". Besides these two concepts, the common denominator that has made "market wizards" so successful is having a high percentage of winning trades and being able to pick the "right" stock or ignoring a losing trade.

Following is a mathematical drawdown rule used by Trend-followers for recovery. The rule is simple, when a trader looses $10,00 out of a total of $10,000 (a 10%-loss), then to recover these loses, there is a need of 11.1% increase on the remaining $9,000. The larger the loss, the greater profit must be obtained to recover.

Figure 4

Drawdown Effects	
Size of drawdown on Initial capital	Percent gain to recover
5%	5,3%
10%	11,1%
15%	17,6%
20%	25,0%
25%	33,3%
30%	42,9%
40%	66,7%
50%	100%
60%	150%
70%	233%
80%	400%
90%	1000%

The importance of cutting losses short is quite logical. If the trader is unable to survive in the markets on a near term basis, then he will not be around when opportunities arise to make money on the long term. Again, the price movement multiplied by position size determines the size of the loss. The greater the number of shares that is, the position size, the greater the loss.

Should a trader sell an asset that is losing money? This is definitely a measure being questioned, as it is difficult to maintain this strategy when there have been down moves from peak to trough of 75% on a stock, by itself representing 40% of the major index when trading at all time high. It is more difficult when the fund managers have been selling the stock the entire journey down. Nevertheless, for those trading the stock markets there is little advise to follow but to buy. The short selling recommendations are very few, as are the recommendations to sell in order to take profits. According to U.S. statistics: of 28,000 recommendations by brokerage-house analysts, 99% of those recommendations on U.S. companies were "strong buy", "buy" or "hold". Only 1% of the time, analysts recommended "sell" (Thomson Financial/First Call Corp., 2001.). Trend-followers sell what shows a loss and keep what shows a profit. This is only the wise thing to do. Generally, traders end up doing just the reverse. Investors and traders, shifting in risk tolerance according to positively and negatively framed situations, show no risk aversion, but an aversion against losses. Loss aversion applies when one is avoiding a loss even if it means accepting a higher risk. The preference for risky actions to avoid an impending loss over less risky options just to minimize the loss and "bite the bullet" can be explained by "loss aversion".

Selling assets that have gained value and keeping assets that have lost value is known as "Disposition effect". The disposition effect is based on two characteristics of prospect theory, namely the tendency of individuals to value gains and losses relatively a reference point and further, the tendency to be risk seeking in situations where a loss might occur and risk averse in situations where a certain gain is possible. Common traders sell their winners and kept their losers finding difficult to adopt the behavior of the "market wizards" or at least avoiding the most flagrant mistakes.

Costs or the losses made at an earlier time may predispose decision-makers to take risks. They are more risk seeking than they would be if they had not made the earlier loss This effect is referred to as "the sunken cost-effect" and results in organizations and individuals "throwing good money after bad" in order to make up for the loss. The loss already incurred makes the context equivalent of a negative frame, but with an increased commitment, for example, buying more shares makes a recovery possible.

On evaluating the market, following assumptions are made:

- People who are aware about position sizing, risk management, and psychological biases lose money to a less extent than people who are unaware.

- People with prior experience of trading/investing will lose money to a less extent than people with less experience.

And the possible factors identified that contributes to the way people decide on position size,

- Prior knowledge of trading/investing

- Risk seeking to diminish with experience (contrary to Prospect theory*)

If lacking enough confidence or capital to start trading, one should spend some time each day performing paper trade analysis. This is a sensible alternative than wasting money on sub-par trading systems or worse, trading with no system at all.

How Much To Buy Or Sell?

We know from the above section that adjusting the size of the risk is the key to successful trading. Risk – too big could make the trader bankrupt; risk – too small gives little possibility to get large profit. The basic rule is clear - how to size a position depends on trader's willingness to take risks, his comfort level with large drawdowns, etc.

With position sizing, Trend-followers believe that in situation that has positive expected value, there is a percentage of one's capital that will give optimal profit. Further, in the years to come, this percentage will give the trader maximum gain. At the same time it should not be ignored that, this percentage may also give the trader very large drawdowns. A smaller position size than "optimal" will give smaller profit but smaller drawdowns. If the player takes even larger positions, then there is a great risk of going bankrupt.

Despite of risk level, it is essential to thoroughly understand how much one is willing to lose in a situation and what the consequences will be for such a loss. For this it is important that we understand the concept and implication of Average True Range.

Average True Range (ATR)

What is a Moving average? A moving average is defined as a method of calculating the average value of a contract's price, or indicator, over a period of time.

How is moving average calculated? A moving average is calculated by mathematically analyzing contract's average value over a predetermined time period (typically 7 days). As the price of contracts changes over time, its average price moves up or down.

True range helps determining and taking decisions on:

- Number of contracts in a unit

- Efficient usage of Stops

- When is it appropriate to add additional units

There are few other factors that should be kept in mind when making decisions based on ATR:

- It peaks just before the price bottoms.

- It also peaks just before the market top.

- It peaks after a secondary rally and also during the early stages of a major price fall.

- Low ATR implies that the market is ranging.

Generally a panic sell-off is followed by ATR values often occur at market bottoms. Also, low ATR values are found during extended sideways periods, such as those found at tops and after consolidations.

Moving Average can be calculated using following formula:

MA (TR, Type, Period)
TR = MAX {ABS (HI - LO), ABS (HI -CL.1), ABS (CL.1 -LO)}

Price difference is another factor that helps traders to understand TR better. The True Range indicator is the greatest of the price difference from:

- Today's high to today's low

- Yesterday's close to today's high

- Yesterday's close to today's low

ATR – an illustration

ATR is a truly adaptive and universal measure of market price movement. Here is an example that illustrates its flexibility.

An example would be: Average price movement (or volatility) of Contract 1 over a two-day period is $500. Average price movement of Contract 2 is about $2,000. Now if we invent a generalized technique to identify appropriate stop losses in both the Contracts, it would have to generate two very different stop levels because of the difference in volatility. So we require a technique that would identify a $750 stop loss in Contract 1 and a $3,000 stop loss in Contract 2. Lets us see how can we do this.

Using the information in the example, the ATR of Contract 1 over a two-day period is $500 and the ATR of Contract 2 over the same period is $2,000. If we use a stop expressed as 1.5 ATR, we could use the same formula for both markets. The Contract 1 stop would be $750 and Contract 2 stop would be $3,000.

Let consider if the market condition changes:

- Contract 1 becomes extremely volatile and moves $1,000 over a two-day period, and

- Contract 2 gets very quiet and now moves only $1,000 over this two-day period.

Using the stops as originally expressed (not using the technique), we would still have a $750 stop in Contract 1 and a $3,000 stop in Contract 2. However, the stop expressed in units of ATR would adapt to the changes, and the new "ATR stops" of 1.5 ATR would translate to $1,500 for both contracts. Further, we can strategically react to the new volatility and use these stops.

The ATR stops automatically adjust to market changes. The new stop is 1.5 ATR; the formula is always the same. The value of using ATR as a universal and adaptive measure of market volatility cannot be overemphasized. ATR is an invaluable tool in building trading systems that are robust, as they are likely to work the same way in the future and can be applied to many markets without modification.

Using ATR, one might be able to build a system for Contract 1 that actually works also in Contract 2, with the same formula. But perhaps more important, one can build a system using ATR that works well over your historical data, regardless of dramatic price fluctuations.

Also it is important for a trader to calculate Unit risk involved that will directs him to add/maintain/subtract his trading position. Unit Risk can be calculated, in a given situation where a unit is his 2% risk in ATR. One unit can consist of 2 ATR. If a trader is long 5 units and short 4 units, take the smaller number (4) and divide it by 2, subtract that number from the larger (5). In this case: 5 -(4/2)=3. This is his Unit risk. Hence, according to the max 10-unit system rule, he can still add 7 more positions, if there are signals of trend developments AND available risk capital warrants it.

Position Trading and the True Range

As we know from the previous section that an Average True Range is determined using the formula given below:

ATR = [(I/15)(today s TR) + (14/15)(prior ATR)]

We know that the price of a contract cannot be static, by calculating ATR we determine the average price movement that may move moves up or down.

Trend-followers understand that Average True Range consists of variable moving average and volume adjusted moving average that automatically adjusts its weighting based on market conditions. Further, we need to understand how to calculate a 21-day moving average of a security. The calculation involves following easy steps.

- The closing prices of a contract are added (X) for the last 21 days
- Average price of that contract (Y) for last 21 days is then calculated by diving the sum (X) by 21
- The average price is plotted on a chart
- Repeat the above three steps for next 21 days
- We have the 21-day moving average of a contract.

Further, let us understand how to calculate a 6% exponential moving average of a contract:

- The closing price of the current day is multiplied by 6%.
- The sum is added to previous day's moving average
- Multiply the value by 94% (100% - 6% _ 94 %).

M.A. = [(Today's close) x 0.06] + [(yesterday's M.A.) x 0.94]

The basic fact is to maximize profits a person must be willing to give up some part of his accumulated profits, by doing this he would be on his way to successful trading. Example: An account is started at $50,000. The market soon takes off and the account swells to $80,000. Many people will quickly pull their $30,000 profit off the table. Their misconception is that if they don't take these profits immediately, they will be gone. Refusing to give up a part of that accumulated income is their big mistake.

Position Traders understand the nature of the market. They realize that $50,000 account may go to $80, 000, back to $55,000 and back up to $90,000, perhaps all the way up to $200,000. This is the consequence of taking the accumulating income? Even people who took profits at $80,000 were not around to take the ride up to $200,000 account.

If a trader is one of those people with a $30, 000 gain in his account. He must be willing to let some of those profits go back to his original sum of $50,000. Instead of protecting his entire $30,000, he is more aggressive, knowing that if he takes his entire profit, he will be forever in the back of the pack with average returns.

How to Pyramid and Move-up Stops Properly using ATR

Pyramiding is defined as using profits from a current market position to purchase additional contracts. The winning trades are expected to have a large "geometric" gain, due to pyramiding and catching a long trending move. The winning positions are expected to more than offset the many smaller losses.

It is safe to pyramid when the initial position is larger than the subsequent position size added. As the price level gradually moves as expected, the size added decreases. This is the reason why it is known as Pyramiding. The example below shows how to add units in a given position once enough profits are built up to pyramid.

Figure 5

Unit accumulation Risk Exposure in ATR	Price	Final Stop level	New profits needed to pyramid
2 ATR	X(initial price)	X	1/2 ATR
2 ATR + 1 1/2 ATR	X+1/2 ATR	X+1/2 ATR	1 ATR
2 ATR + 1 1/2 ATR + 1	X+1 ATR	X+1 ATR	1 1/2 ATR
2 ATR + 1 1/2 ATR + 1 + 1/2	X+1 1/2 ATR	X+1 1/2 ATR	2 ATR
2 ATR + 1 1/2 ATR + 1 + 1/2	X+2 ATR	X+2 ATR	2 1/2 ATR
2 ATR + 1 1/2 ATR + 1 + 1/2	X+2 1/2 ATR	X+2 1/2 ATR	3 ATR
2 ATR + 1 1/2 ATR + 1 + 1/2	X+3 ATR	X+2 1/2 ATR	3 1/2 ATR
2 ATR + 1 1/2 ATR + 1 + 1/2	X+3 1/2 ATR	X+2 1/2 ATR	4 ATR
2 ATR + 1 1/2 ATR + 1 + 1/2	X+4 ATR	X+2 1/2 ATR	4 1/2 ATR
2 ATR + 1 1/2 ATR + 1 + 1/2	X+4 1/2 ATR	X+2 1/2 ATR	5 ATR

Speculators must have 1/2 ATR gains to move up to the next unit. Looking at the chart, we realize that the forth unit there is a 5 ATR risk in place and there is a 2 ATR risk in place after the first unit is purchased.

Position Traders aim to pyramid early in a trend. The reason behind this is when pyramiding further into a trend the losses can be large when there is a reversal. One does not want a trade that reaches 20 ATR and have the average price at entry be 12 ATR, that s asking for serious trouble and loss.

When trading like Trend-followers, it is desirable that traders place all units between 4 ATR and 6 ATR. After 6 ATR they assume that the danger is ahead, if pyramiding is continued. Trend-followers use 2 ATR range. If a 2 ATR range goes against as expected, then the trader moves out. This is considered the money management stop and very vital in our trading system.

One money management rule, following the rules of our school of thought, is to increase the number of contracts as the number of false breakouts increases. This is because false breakouts occur during periods of market consolidation and large moves occur on breakouts from long periods of consolidation. Another effective money management rule for a channel breakout system is to decrease the number of contracts after every large winning trade. If a person has $ 50,000 per contract winning trade on a contract, then he would drop back to one contract until the market consolidates again.

Trend-followers consider getting out of losing trade acceptable as long as a signal with more expectation exists. All this comes through experience and an intuitive understanding of the rules is also important.

System Parameters & Equity Curve

As we know that Position Trading adapts to different markets and different market conditions, the system is based on keeping things proportional to the market's volatility. This ability to adapt to changing volatility (the market's ups and downs) is built into the core of any successful trend follower's system.

During a volatile period, a good Position Trading system will dictate that a person trades less contracts or shares. During periods of lower volatility, the system allows you to trade more contracts or shares. In other words, commitments are increased during favorable risk/reward periods and decreased during less favorable periods.

The system rules are the same for each market. Computer technology can be easily used to over-optimize a trading system and produce something that looks good. By testing thousands of possibilities, one can create a system that works.

The system parameters or rules work across a range of values. System parameters that work over a range of values are robust. When the parameters of a system are slightly changed, the performance adjusts drastically. For example, if a system works great at 25, but does not work at 24 or 26, this implies that system has poor robustness. On the other hand, if the system parameter is 50 and it also works at 40 or 60, then the system is much more robust and very importantly reliable.

Traders often focus only on future profits when looking at a system. The key, however, is risk control (or money management). If a trader controls his risks and runs his profits, he could position himself to make bigger money throughout the long term.

A good system with robust and adaptive parameters should not require re-optimization. Our system uses indicators and parameters that adapt to changing market conditions.

Let us consider an example. Given:
- Starting account = $100,000 (100%)
- Maximum risk per unit = $2000 (2%)
- One unit = the number of contracts in a market equivalent to $1000 in equity change given a 1 ATR price movement.

Now, if 1 ATR = $200 in equity change per contract, then 1 unit is equivalent to 5 contracts. Following this a speculator can determine how many units should be allowed in their portfolios.

Position Traders generally, limit their portfolios to 10 total units, or 20 units if longs are balances against shorts. In other words, 10 dependent units are equal to 5 independent units. Please refer to the Portfolio diversification unit of this book to understand this in details.

Trend-followers can enhance the way they trade through the use of equity curve management strategies. These techniques, has periods of ups and downs in terms of performance. Once a trader begins trading as a *Smart Money*, he develops an equity curve. Once he has an equity curve, he can begin to trade it in such a fashion to reduce risk and enhance return. The key factors for all the traders are quantifying the exact equity level of the account, including run-up and drawdown.

In periods of losing (with the equity curve turning up), adding proportionally one additional position across markets is a good start. In periods of winning (with the equity curve turning down), subtracting proportionally one additional position across markets is a good start.

Equity curve trading is absolutely the last step of the trading process. Our method of speculating is not a curve fit system. Curve fit systems customize the trading rules differently for each trading market, producing unrealistic results.

Equity Curve Trading

Once the speculator gets beyond the dry statistical language of these subjects the faster the overall understanding of the importance of these issues will sink in. You do not need to be a math major or have an advanced degree in mathematics to understand and adopt these notions.

So what is equity curve trading? Once the speculator has developed a record in terms of equity growth in a portfolio the equity can be charted and assigned Moving Averages. These Moving Averages are the same as discussed in the technical analysis section of this book. Equity Curve Trading is a money management technique that can sometimes improve investing performance by modifying the position sizing based on crossovers of a moving average of the equity curve.[1]

There are several ways of approaching this. If you are a person who appreciates casino gambling there is an analogy can be drawn to gaming. The bankroll a prudent gambler allocates to recreational gambling should never hinder his or hers lifestyle and the kids education. Similarly in investments one must draw the line in losing positions when one adjust portfolio positions. In some styles of equity curve trading the self-imposed rules call for stop trading when the equity curve is below a certain Moving Average and only resume trading when the equity curve moves above such threshold.

The other, more advanced technique is adjusting the unit size and exposure (portfolio heat) when running into a losing streak.

Trading Losses And Profits

Why does not everybody minimize losses and maximize profits? Traditionally, economic theory is based on the idea that market is rational and therefore makes rational decisions. Feelings and biases do not influence the investor's judgment, only relevant information affects their behavior. Decision-makers decide on basis of the probability of each alternative outcome and select the alternative giving the maximum return. This view is not supported without exception.

Some common mistakes that a trader commits are discussed below:

Costs, that is, losses, made at an earlier time may predispose decision-makers to take risks. They are more risk seeking than they would be if they had not made the earlier loss. The loss already incurred makes the context equivalent of a negative frame, but with an increased commitment, for example, buying more shares makes a recovery possible, although uncertain.

Situation framing also affects trader's decision. Investors and traders, shifting in risk tolerance according to positively and negatively framed situations, show no risk aversion, but an aversion against losses. Loss aversion applies when one is avoiding a loss even if it means accepting a higher risk. The preference for risky actions to avoid an impending loss over less risky options just to minimize the loss and bite the bullet can be explained by 'loss aversion'.

Negative games may cause a trader to go broke. In a negative expectancy game, there is no money management scheme. If a trader continues to bet, regardless of how he manages his money, it is almost certain that he will be a loser.
So it is advisable to bet when a trader has a positive expectancy. A positive expectation does not mean overtrading; it means that the trader has an edge.

Keeping what shows loss and selling what shows profit is one of the common mistakes committed by the trader. Always sell what shows a loss and keep what shows a profit. Most of

---

[1] Article by Michael R. Bryant in www.adaptrade.com/Articles/article-eq.htm

the time people end up doing just the reverse. It has been described that selling assets that have gained value and keeping assets that have lost value as Disposition effect. The disposition effect is based on two characteristics of prospect theory, namely the tendency of individuals to value gains and losses relatively a reference point and further, the tendency to be risk seeking in situations where a loss might occur and risk averse in situations where a certain gain is possible. The first goal is to survive in short term in order to be able to make gains in the long run.

Remember:

- A loss of 2% requires a gain of 3% on remaining capital in order to break even.

- A loss of 30% requires a gain of 43% on remaining capital in order to break even.

- A loss of 50% requires a gain of 100% on remaining capital in order to break even.

- A loss of 90% requires a gain of 1000% on remaining capital in order to break even.

The importance of cutting losses short is obvious. Large losses can be avoided if the trader only risks a small amount of capital in each and every trade and not letting a streak of losses compound into a big portion of initial capital.

Mathematical Expectation

It would not be wrong if we say that mathematical expectation is the foundation of the Speculator's successful approach to the markets. A positive winning expectation is mandatory to be present when *smart money* enters a market. Said in other words a trader may loose money if he enters the market with a negative expectation. One of the most important of our trading rule is to let the profits run, doing that a trader should feel comfortable wagering money with this positive expectation.

The first and foremost money management rule of letting the profits run is understood but the question is how much to wager in a given positive mathematical expectation. No doubt, much of this depends on the risk taking ability of an individual.

Example: In a given situation where there is a 50% chance to win 10 and a 50% chance of losing 3, the expected return would be 3.5. Stated the other way, for every game one plays where one have these odds he could expect to make 3.5 each and every play on average over the long run.

The formula is: [(PP) (P)] - [(PP) (L)] = E (R)

Where:

P = Profit

L = Loss

PP = Percent Probability

E (R) = Expected Rate of Return

Figure 6

1	PP=1/2	P=1	L=1	E(R)=0
2	PP=1/2	P=3	L=1	E(R)=1
3	PP=1/2	P=7	L=2	E(R)=2.5
4	PP=1/2	P=10	L=3	E(R)=3.5

There is a 50% chance of winning or losing; it does not matter if one loses 50% of the time as long as he is making more when he wins. One advantage with our system is that the risk level among speculators varies depending upon the size of the profit they seek.

Short term trading is not, by definition, less risky. Some people may mistakenly apply a cause and effect relationship between using a long-term strategy and the potential of incurring large loss. They forget profit and loss is proportional. A short-term system will never allow to be in the trend long enough to achieve large profits. A trader may end up with small losses but also small profits. Added together, numerous small losses equal a big loss.

When trading for the long term, the trader has a more positive expectation in terms of the size of the move. In the big picture, the larger the move, the larger the validation of the move.

If trading some short-term pattern predictive system a trader would never be able to participate fully in the big trends. Big trends make the big profits. Prudent speculating for the long-term places far less emphasis on perfect fills for success. In contrast, short term traders' transaction costs and skids on their fills affect their bottom line to a much greater degree.
Lets us understand factors that affect a person's decision-making and Profit-Loss in Smart Investing.

Streaks/Gamblers Fallacy

When probability of winning is 50%, then there will be an equal number of wins and losses over a large number of draws. A common misconception is that this distribution will be maintained after every draw, that is, a winner will follow after a loser has been drawn. However, in a big sample of draws where the odds are 50/50 it is neither impossible nor uncommon to find a streak of 7 - 10 draws of equal value (e.g. a streak of losses). In such situation, using a Martingale-strategy (doubling the bet after each loss) could be a catastrophe. The streak of losses puts the gambler in a "sunken cost" situation, where he/she may become more risk seeking.

Prospect theory"/"Disposition Effects

Psychological research has found that most individuals are risk seeking when the situation at hand is perceived as a losing situation and risk-averse when the situation is perceived as a winning situation. We decide in accordance with "Prospect theory". We tend to keep our losers and sell our winners.

R – multiples

"R" is the size of the risk in our ongoing or planned market position. Our losing trades should be small R-multiples and our winning trades large R-multiples. A low "hit-rate" (probability of winning/losing) with large winners and small losers (e.g. 10R winners and 1R losers) is preferable to a high probability of winning with small winners and big losers.

Expectancy/ expected value

Having a 50% probability of a 2R winner and a 1R loss or 25% probability of a 6R winner and a 75% probability of a 1R loss? (The 0.5*2 – 0.5*1 =0.5 in contrast to 0.25*6 – 0.75*1 = 0.75 is the difference).

The rational investor exists in theory.

A basic knowledge of computing the possibility of a certain gain is essential. The expected value is one of the most important statistical-parameters in contrast to probability of winning. When the trader is capable of computing the expected value, then he/she is in the position to estimate when the odds are in his/her favor.

Comparison with Alternate Money Management Scheme

New Position Risk

- Decide the trade entry price according to the trading system.

- Establish the stop-loss price. Calculate the price difference between the entry point and the stop-loss point in terms of dollars per contract.

- Example: If you buy gold at $400 per oz., with stop at $390 (trailing with a 10-day moving average of closing prices), account size will be: $200,000. (400 390) x $100/point = $1,000 risk per contract.

- Establish the risk per trade in percentage equity terms i.e., $200,000 x 1 % = $2,000 per trade.

- Risk per trade divided by risk per contract will determine the number of contracts to buy for the position.

- In this case risk per trade/$1,000 risk per contract = $2000/$1000 per trade = 2 contracts

Ongoing Risk Exposure

- Calculate the risk limit per existing trade in percentage equity terms, e.g. 2.5%.

- Establish the risk per contract on the basis of the changes in price and stop-loss point. (450-405) x $100/point = $4,500

- Portfolio equity determines risk that is to allowed ($210,000 x 2.5% = 5,250)

- After determining the allowable risk it is divided by risk contract. This gives the number of contracts to hold. $5,250/$4,500 = 1.167

Daily Volatility

- You should have the open, high, low, and closing prices of the last two trading days.

- Market's true range - price movement over the last 24-hour trading period is determined. This is done by out the difference between the higher of yesterday's close vs. the lower of yesterday's close or today's high vs. today's low.

- True range in ticks is converted into dollars.

- Average daily volatility is determined. $3 average true range x $100 per point = $300 average volatility per contract.

- Average these figures for a period of time, say for example 10 days.

- Risk per position is divided by average volatility per contract. This gives the number of contracts to hold.

($200,000 x 1 %)/$300 = 6.67 contracts (round down to 6 contracts).

You may compare this with the result as determined by the ongoing risk exposure and take the lower of the two. Dependence on volatility and appropriate account size are vital factors that help a trader to determine proper portfolio to trade. The main reason for volatility controls is for the psychological benefit. If you have too much volatility in any one position it attracts your attention. Your focus shifts to one particular position and you can lose sight of the big picture. By controlling volatility you always adjust risk exposure and keep yourself psychologically balanced. We have already discussed why appropriate account size and position sizing is important.

Risk Control By Analyzing Size, Risk/Reward Ratio, And Percent Accuracy

We all agree that markets would not exist without loosing traders. Their trading losses fund the winning traders who make prices efficient and provide liquidity. So, controlling risk becomes extremely important while trading.

One may find this weird but the truth is that winning traders can only profit to the extent that other traders are willing to lose. Traders are willing to take risk and lose when they obtain external benefits from trading. Hence, the cycle continues.

The external benefits are returns that are expected from holding risky securities that represent deferred consumption. External benefits can also be availed by hedging and gambling.

As stated earlier in unit I, our decisions are influenced by how a situation is framed. When the options at hand generally have a perceived probability to result in a positive outcome it is framed positively. Negative framing occurs when the perceived probability weighs over into a negative outcome scenario. Example: In an experiment, the participants were to choose one of two scenarios, 80% possibility to win $ 4,000 and the 20% risk of not winning anything as opposed to a 100% possibility of winning $ 3,000. Although the riskier choice had a higher expected value ($ 4,000 x 0.8 = $ 3,200), 80% of the participants chose the safe $ 3,000. When participants had to choose between 80% possibility to loose $ 4,000 and the 20% risk of not losing anything as one scenario, and a 100% possibility of losing $ 3,000 as the other scenario, 92% of the participants picked the gambling scenario. This framing effect occurs because traders over-weight losses when they are described as definitive, as opposed to situations where they are described as possible. People tend to fear losses more than they value gains. A $ 1 loss is more painful than the pleasure of a $ 1 gain.

In the above example, describing a loss as certain, it has created the effect more painful. As a result, it inflicted on investor's decision trying to avoid such a loss. Consequently, they will take a greater risk and gamble in a losing situation, holding on to the position in hope that prices will recover. In a winning situation the circumstances are reversed. Investors will become risk averse and quickly take profits, not letting profits run. Our system realizes this and gears up the reader for any such mind frames.

The biggest challenge is to know where the market is going. *Smart Money* trades for the outsized large move. Several big trends a year are key to success. The strategy cuts losing positions quickly. Consequently, a few big trades make up the bulk of profits and many small trades make up the losses. Winning trades can range from 35-50%, but that percentage reveals little information since we expect more losses (of smaller value) than winners (of much larger value). Win/loss ratio, while a favorite of the novice trader, is useless in terms of the trend-follower's analysis.

The Position Traders use a 2% money management stop on each position they take, so they limit risk to 2% of their capital. The concept of the Trend-followers sitting out the next signal if the prior position was a winner is an important aspect of the entry signal process. If the last trade within the system was a loss, initiation at the current signal has more positive mathematical expectation.

Even if the last trade was a loss on a short position, the next signal, even if it is a long signal, still has greater expectation.

Trading in units allow an easy way to manage risk and control equity. Units are constantly adjusting based on account equity.

Money management should generally employ 3 basic principles of loss prevention. Units can be used to determine:

- Percent of equity trading size on will risk, i.e. 2% of equity is maximum stop loss.

- Money Management stop would typically involve volatility units. I.e. 2-volatility stop loss.
- Volatility stop would involve an increase in volatility, i.e. % increase in volatility units.

On comparing monthly standard deviations (volatility as measured from the mean) and semi-standard deviations (volatility measured on the downside only) it was found that while Trend-followers experience a lot of volatility, it is concentrated on the upside, not the downside. Most Trend-followers' volatility is on the plus side or they would not be in business. The difference between the standard deviation and the semi-standard deviation is what counts.

The actual formula for calculating them is identical, with one exception: the semi-standard deviation looks only at observations below the mean. If the semi-standard deviation is lower than the standard deviation, the historical pull away from the mean has to be on the plus side. If it is higher, it means the pull away from the mean is on the minus side.

The Position Trading method's ability to adapt to different markets and different market conditions is based on keeping things proportional to the market's volatility. The ability to adapt to changing volatility (or said another way the market's ups and downs) is built into the core of the Position Trading system. Trades are increased during favorable risk/reward periods and decreased during less favorable periods.

Assumptions:
1. Starting account = $500,000
2. Equity unit = 2.5%
3. Risk of ruin = 30 equity units in a row

This proves that an equity unit is a concept directly related to risk of ruin. The estimated equity required per one contract to trade is the multiplied value of Volatility Units and the Risk of Ruin. In this example, one would need $37,200 to trade Corn, $93,000 for Deutsche Mark, $97,500 for Gold and would need $227,700 to trade all 3 contracts together in a portfolio. Hence, in this case, 30 losing trades in a row will equal ruin.

Figure 7

	Corn	Deutsche Mark	Gold
Given:			
One Volatility Unit in Ticks	30	80	100
Money Management Stop in Ticks	80	100	130
Dollars Per Tick	$15.50	$31	$25.00
Unknowns			
Volatility Units (Money Management Stop in Ticks/One Volatility Unit in Ticks)	80/30=2.67	100/80=1.25	130/100 = 1.3
Volatility Units Required (Money Management Stop in Ticks x Dollars Per Tick)	(80)(15.50)=$1240	(100)(31)=$3100	(130)(25)=$3250
Equity Unit ($) based on 2.5% of $500,000 (Starting Account) Trading Unit	$12,500	$12,500	$12,500
Equity Unit/Volatality Unit	12500/1240=10.05	12500/3100=4.03	12500/3250=3.84
Equity Needed Per (1) contract traded (Volatility Units Required) (40)	($1240)(30) = $37,200	($3100)(30)=$93,000	($3250)(30)=$97,500

Even a profitable methodology has some calculated risks as well as some losses. Position Trading s is a function of the risk level desired. Risk level among traders varies depending upon the size of the profit they seek. For example, if a trader looks at 100%+ a year gains then he must be prepared for the possibility of a 30%.

As mentioned earlier, it is important for a trader to calculate Unit risk involved that will directs him to add/maintain/subtract his trading position. Unit Risk can be calculated, in a given situation where a unit is his 2% risk in ATR. One unit can consist of 2 ATR. If a trader is long 5 units and short 4 units, take the smaller number (4) and divide it by 2, subtract that number from the larger (5). In this case: 5 -(4/2)=3. This is his Unit risk. Hence, according to the max 10-unit rule, he can still add 7 more positions, if there are signals of trend developments AND available risk capital warrants it.

Trend Traders operate under the theory that extreme strength leads to more strength, and extreme weakness leads to more weakness. So it is advisable that one should not buy the dips, or average the losses. This trading principle goes against the consumer society, but Trend-followers believe in cutting losses and letting their profits run.

Long-term success in any of these probabilistic exercises shares some common features.

- Lots of situations. Players of probabilistic games must examine lots of situations, because the "market" price is usually pretty accurate. Investors, too, must evaluate lots of situations and gather lots of information.

- Limited opportunities. Even if a trader plays under ideal circumstances, the odds still favor him less than 10% of the time. And rarely does anyone play under ideal circumstances. The message for investors is even when you are competent, favorable situations—where you have a clear-cut variant perception vis-à-vis the market—don't appear very often.

- Ante. Ideally, a trader can bet a small amount when the odds are poor and a large sum when the odds are favorable, but a good player must ante to play the game. In investing, on the other hand, a trader need not participate when he perceives the expected value as unattractive, and he can bet aggressively when a situation appears attractive.

Constantly thinking in expected value terms requires discipline and is somewhat unnatural. But the leading thinkers and practitioners from somewhat varied fields have converged on the same formula: focus not on the frequency of correctness, but on the magnitude of correctness.

The key is to wait for a good opportunity and then take advantage of it. A good opportunity is when a person observes the market well and keeps his investments in line with the moving trend. Another opportunity occurs when developing pattern is observed. The idea is to minimize the losses.

Money and risk management, plus diversification in Position Trading, are interwoven with trend trading. There are rather long periods in which no ascertainable trends can be seen in a given market. This period eventually passes and some trend manages to re-establish itself.

Position Trading mandates that we wait for these periods to pass and not trade until a strong trend is observed.

Position Trading adapts to different markets and different market conditions. The system is based on keeping things proportional to the market's volatility. This ability to adapt to changing volatility (the market's ups and downs) is built into the core of any successful trend follower's system.

During a volatile period, a good Position Trading system dictates that a trader trades less contracts or shares. During periods of lower volatility, the system allows a trader to trade more contracts or shares. In other words, commitments are increased during favorable risk/reward periods and decreased during less favorable periods. The main reason for volatility controls is for the psychological benefit. If a trader has too much volatility in any one position it attracts his attention. This shifts his focus shifts to one particular position and then he could loose sight of the big picture. By controlling volatility a person can adjust risk exposure and can keep himself psychologically balanced.

Position Trading Rules

Position Traders are advised to:

- Not to risk more than 1% of their account per trade.

- Not to expose their account more than 2 ATR risk at any time while trading.

- Wait for a trade to move to breakeven before they add new trades.

- Trade the strongest commodity; an example may be grains and currencies.

- Trade when the volatility shrinks (when it is down, it allows more contracts to be used for the same dollar risk).

- Limited their account to a total of 10 units, 5 units in any one market with a 2 ATR stop loss is an ideal set-up.

- Make approximately 1/2 ATR average profit on all previous units.

- Make decisions considering that the total profits in all other positions do not bear relevance to individual market decisions.

- Not to increase trading volume with increasing equity.

- Avoid trading close to 1/3 ATR before a breakout or 1/2 ATR after it.

- Not let a market go to 10 ATR, as that would make their average entry price be 6 ATR.

- Try to have all units on by 4 ATR, 6 ATR at the latest.

- Count 6 ATR from the break out point, yet this may not be the entry price point of the daily bar breakout that signaled the position.

- Try to have majority of units on before 6 ATR, because from initiation point to 3 ATR there is roughly the same expectation of trend strength. After 6 ATR the expectation falls off.

- Approach entry, exit, pyramiding, liquidation, and stops in fraction.

- Remember 90% of trends end after 10 ATR.

Besides the rules given above, it is very important to catch a great trend that might not be as simple as one might assume. Without inflation on the horizon, futures will tend to have trendless, sideways markets. High-volume breakout, coupled with price breakout, AND open-interest increases can help establish a true trending market. The next chapters deal with this in detail.

Overall Money Management

If a person has a finely tuned money management strategies and a trading system best suited to his needs, he will still need a methodology to judge his trading results. This can be done by statistically analyzing the results in terms with his expected returns. Trading efficiency and Profitability are after trade measurements that are crucial for keeping track of success or failure.

Trading efficiency is measured by

[(Total profits - total losses)/# trades]/[(total profits + total losses)/# trades]. A trading edge above 0% is profitable.

Profitability is measured by -

(% Profitable trades x average profit)/(% unprofitable trades x average loss)
A profit factor that is greater than 1 is profitable.

Expected Trade is measured by -

(% Profitable x % average profitable) - (% unprofitable x % average unprofitable)
An expected trade greater than 0 is profitable.

Net Trade is measured by -

(Total profits - total losses - commissions)/# trades
A net trade greater than 0 is profitable.

In the end, it should be understood that markets do not change. Markets behave the same as they did 300 hundred years ago. The hopes and desires of men and women who trade the markets are manifested in trending behavior. The trick is to trade a method that takes advantage of major market moves. Markets are the same today because they always change. The key is to trade a system that responds to change. If you have a philosophy that's sound, you're going to be able to take advantage of those changes to greater or lesser degrees. It is the same with using good, sound business principles, the changing world is not going to materially hurt you if your principles are designed to adapt. This is precisely why Prudent Speculating continues to win.

The Futures Markets

Before Mastery - Chop Wood Carry Water
After Mastery - Chop Wood Carry Water

Futures markets can be described as continuous auction markets and as clearinghouses for the latest supply and demand information.

The meeting places of buyers and sellers, the Futures market today includes an ever-expanding list of commodities such as: agricultural products, metals, petroleum, financial instruments, foreign currencies and stock indexes.

The futures market continues to grow and diversify rapidly. Though the future's contract trading volume increased from 14 million in 1970 to 179 million in 1985, yet their primary purpose remains the same as it has been for nearly a century - to provide a successful mechanism to manage price risks.

Who are the futures market participants? They are Speculative investors who accept the risks that others avoid. With no intention of taking delivery of the commodity, speculators they seek profit from a change in the price. In other words, they buy when they anticipate rising prices and sell when they anticipate declining prices.

The interaction of investors and speculators has helped to provide active, liquid and competitive markets. And with the availability of alternative methods of participation, speculative participation in futures trading has become even more attractive.

Only a relatively small amount of money is required to control assets having a much greater value, but everyone cannot be comfortable with speculation in futures contracts. This is due to the possibility of large profits or losses in relation to the initial commitment of capital that stems principally from the fact that futures' trading is a highly leveraged form of speculation. The leverage of futures trading works in favor when prices move in the anticipated direction or against when prices move in the opposite direction.

Master Speculators understand that an intelligent allocation to futures trading can provide greater diversification and a higher rate of return. There are a number of ways in which one can use futures in combination with stocks, bonds and other investments. This has been discussed later in the book.

History of Futures Trading

Since the beginning of the mid-nineteenth century the futures market has been in existence in the U.S. Almost exclusively, grain producers and dealers have been using them to check adverse price movements. As the time passed, the volume of the contracts traded increased and a third group of the market participants started assuming the risk transferred. This group consisted of the Speculators. Speculators had no interest in underlying commodity, but actively traded the contracts to profit from price changes.

There was substantial growth in Futures trading in the late nineteenth and the early twentieth century. The establishment of new exchanges introduced a variety of different commodity contracts over the years.

In 1971, the U.S ended the gold standard. As a result it was projected that the fixed currency rates fluctuations policy would also come to an end. Due to the change in global financial structure, the futures industry began to expand its contract offering to allow financial institution to hedge their currency risk.

In 1972, the Chicago Mercantile Exchange introduced futures on seven foreign currencies and created world's first financial future contracts.

In 1973, this became even more appealing to institutions as the western countries allowed currency rates to float free.

In late 1970's, the interest rates – and in 1982 stock index futures were launched and trading expanded rapidly into many new financial futures instruments.

These developments opened a new dimension in global opportunities. A new type of trader emerged, that applied new trading concepts. Consequently, a sophisticated future trading was launched. Over a period of time these traders started to manage other people's assets and emerged as new, major market participants.

The need to manage price and interest rate risks is increasing in virtually every type of modern business. The futures market is no different. Today the future markets have become major financial markets. The participants include mortgage bankers as well as farmers, bond dealers as well as grain merchants, and multinational corporations as well as food processors, savings and loan associations, and individual speculators.

Now that it is understood what futures markets are, why they exist, the next step is to understand various ways that enables a trader to participate in futures trading.

You Can Trade Your Own Account

- You make your own trading decisions.

- You assure that adequate funds are promptly provided as needed.

- Individual trading account can be opened either directly with a Futures Commission Merchant or indirectly through an Introducing Broker.

Have Someone Manage Your Account

- A managed account is also an individual account, but you give an account manager written power of attorney to make and execute decisions about what and when to trade.

- You remain fully responsible for any losses that may incur

- You remain responsible for meeting margin calls, including making up any deficiencies that exceed your margin deposits.

- No sharing of gains or losses of other customers.

- Many Futures Commission Merchants and Introducing Brokers accept managed accounts.

Using a Commodity Trading Advisor

- Commodity Trading Advisor - an individual or firm - for a fee provides advice on commodity trading (when to establish a particular long or short position and when to liquidate that position, etc.)

- Advisors offer analyses and judgments as to the prospective rewards and risks of the trades they suggest.

- The account remains with a Futures Commission Merchant and in your name, with the advisor designated in writing to make and execute trading decisions on a discretionary basis.

Commodity Pool

- The concept is similar to a common stock mutual fund.

- You do not have your own individual trading account.

- Your money is combined with that of other pool participants and, in effect, traded as a single account.

- Profits or losses of the pool are shared in proportion to your investment in the pool.

- Advantage is greater diversification of risks.

- Your risk of loss is generally limited to your investment in the pool, because most pools are formed as limited partnerships.

What To Look For In A Futures Contract

Trading futures contracts can affect investment results, so they should be properly understood while making investment decisions.

The Contract Unit

- Delivery-type futures contracts lay down the specifications of the commodity to be delivered. Example: 6,000 bushels of grain, 50,000 pounds of livestock, or 500 troy ounces of gold

- Foreign currency futures provide for delivery of a specified number of currencies. Example: marks, francs, yen, pounds or pesos.

- U.S. Treasury obligation futures are in terms of instruments having a stated face value, example: $100,000 or $1 million at maturity.

Choosing A Futures Contract

- The supply and demand uncertainties could suddenly propel prices sharply higher or sharply lower

- Supply and demand depends on future developments.

- Evaluation and choosing the futures contracts, based on present information, can meet trader's objectives and his willingness to accept risk.

How Prices Are Quoted

Futures prices are usually quoted the same way prices are quoted in the cash market: in dollars, cents, per bushel, pound or ounce; also in dollars, cents and increments of a cent for foreign currencies; and in points and percentages of a point for financial instruments.

Minimum Price Changes

- Exchanges establish the minimum amount that the price can fluctuate upward or downward.

- These minimum price fluctuations are known as the "tick".

- Example, if each tick for grain is 0.25 cents per bushel, then on a 5,000 bushel futures contract, it will be $12.50.

Position Limits

- Stated in number of contracts or total units of the commodity

- Position limits establish limits on the maximum speculative position that any one person can have at one time in any one futures contract.

Daily Price Limits

- Exchanges establish daily price limits, stated in terms of the previous day's closing price plus and minus so many cents or dollars per trading unit.

- It prevents a buyer or a seller from being able to exert undue influence on the price in either the establishment or liquidation of positions.

Understanding (And Managing) The Risks Of Futures Trading

Traders buying or selling futures contracts should know that the Risks of any given transaction might result in a Futures Trading loss.

Timing

- Anticipate the timing of price changes

- An adverse price change may, in the short run, result in a greater loss than a trader is willing to accept in the hope of eventually being proven right in the long run.

Liquidity

- There is no assurance that a liquid market will exist for redeeming a futures contract that you have previously bought or sold.

- Two useful indicators of liquidity are the volume of trading and the open interest.

Spreads

- Gains and losses occur only as the result of a change in the price difference, rather than as a result of a change in the overall level of futures prices

- Spreads involve the purchase of one futures contract and the sale of a different futures contract in the hope of profiting from a widening or narrowing of the price difference.

- Spreads are often considered more conservative and less risky than having an outright long or short futures position.

Options On Futures Contracts

- The principal attraction of buying options is that they make it possible to speculate on increasing or decreasing futures prices with a known and limited risk.

- The most that the buyer of an option can lose is the cost of purchasing the option (known as the option "premium") plus transaction costs.

Managed Futures

In contrast to other alternative investment strategies, Managed Future investments performed well during the global liquidity crises of August 1998. The performance of Managed demonstrated their diversification potential and more assets did subsequently flow into the managed Future's market.

Then, 1999 turned out to be one of the worst performing years of the industry. The performance as well as the acceptance of Managed Futures, since then, has improved. As the global stock markets are declining, an increasing number of investors are finding this strategy a good alternative. The following section will take a closer look at this asset class.

Managed futures have grown rapidly in popularity and acceptance in the past decade. Today, there are over $25 million in managed futures accounts. Potentially high returns and their diversification and inflation hedging potential are few of the factors that had led it so far.

The supply and demand conditions determine the prices in the Futures Markets.

More buyers than sellers indicate that the prices will be forced up.
More sellers than buyers indicate that the prices will be forced down.

Prices are actually determined by buy and sell orders originating from all sources that for execution are channeled to the exchange-trading floor. These orders are translated into actual purchases and sales on the exchange-trading floor. This is done by public outcry across the trading ring or pit and not by private negotiation. The prices at which transactions are made are recorded and immediately released for distribution over a vast telecommunications network.

So we now know that a commodity exchanges do not determine or establish the prices at which commodity futures are bought and sold. The purpose of a commodity exchange is just to provide an organized marketplace where members can freely buy and sell various commodities of their choice. Not operating for profit, the exchange merely provides the facilities and ground rules to trade in commodity futures.

Varied Investment Approaches

Commodity Trading Advisors (CTA's) are professional money managers who manage the assts of their clients using derivative instruments, such as futures, forward contracts and options.

As an asset category in the alternative investment industry, Managed Futures can be managed by applying a broad spectrum of different trading models. Three of these trading models are Systematic Model, Discretionary Model and a combination of both.

The most commonly used approach, Systematic Model, allows fully automated trading. Evaluation of the momentum is done by technical analysis and the results: changes in the price and volume etc. are used as input factors.

In contrast, the Non-Systematic or the Discretionary Models applies personal experience and judgment to make decisions. They prefer trading concentrated portfolios and use fundamental data to assess the market. Technical analysis is also used to improve the timing.

The picture below shows the three trading approaches in terms of trading style, time frame, markets traded and analysis.

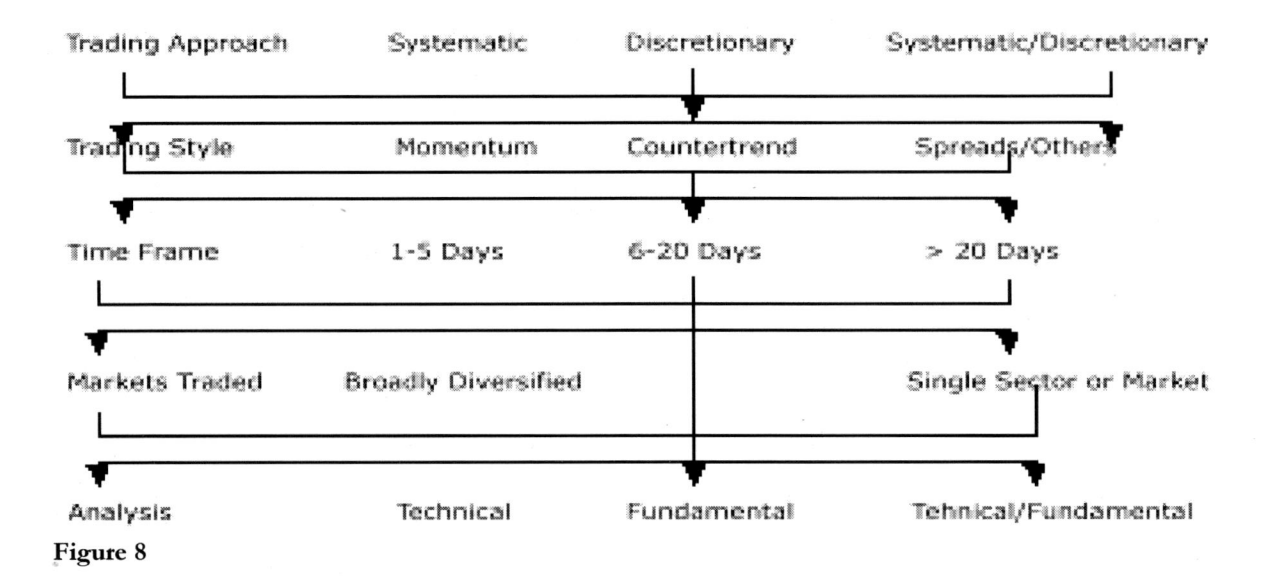

Trading Approach	Systematic	Discretionary	Systematic/Discretionary
Trading Style	Momentum	Countertrend	Spreads/Others
Time Frame	1-5 Days	6-20 Days	> 20 Days
Markets Traded	Broadly Diversified		Single Sector or Market
Analysis	Technical	Fundamental	Tehnical/Fundamental

Figure 8

The Investment Approach - Managed Futures, Stylized Facts and Functionality

Following is a brief description of how this trading system operates, and you would agree this is not rocket science!

Approximately 70% of the CTA's have Systematic Position Trading approach because it generates strong returns in the trending markets. The risk management guidelines of this strategy limit the losses during sideways markets.

Seeking to identify trends across a spectrum of different time frames, systematic Position Traders maintain positions throughout the long-term trends that take place in the markets. The systematic application of quantitative models: moving averages, breakouts of price ranges, or other technical rules to generate the 'buy' and 'sell' signals for a set of markets forms the basis of trading.

In Futures Market multiple models with different entry and exit points can be applied simultaneously and once trade signals are generated, the next crucial aspect is risk management.

Usually between 0.5%-1.5% of the total portfolio equity, the initial risk taken by each trade is determined by the trading system. Protective stops are adjusted daily by adding up more positions if the trends are stable or reducing positions during volatile periods.

Risk control is further achieved by market diversification. Managed Futures are interesting for investors as they provide diversified exposure to wide range of markets in contrast to a traditional investment portfolio consisting primarily of stocks and bonds. Most trend-based CTA's offer globally diversified portfolio of around forty or more markets. The key objective in pursuing portfolio diversification is to avoid experiencing losses in different portfolio components at the same time.

The managed futures trading should be uncorrelated with the other portfolio components. Diversification benefits managed futures, when the non-correlation criterion remains strong. It is possible that two non-correlated investment categories achieve profits over time by pursuing different paths to profitability.

Traditional analysis of managed futures performance is concentrated in comparing managed futures in terms of return and standard deviation, and measuring the risk/return contribution of managed futures indices to a portfolio of traditional assets.

Managed Futures and Stock and Bond Correlation

Historically, Managed Futures have shown low correlation to Bond and Stock market returns. This low correlation is here to stay.

Moves in the price of the currencies may result from economic and political uncertainty that in turn makes a negative impact on the stock market. This creates profit opportunities for the CTA's. Broad diversification of the markets traded is another factor that results in low correlation. The low correlation results in Managed Futures investments to offer the potential to reduce the downside risk of a traditional portfolio during loosing equity periods and improve the overall performance of the portfolio.

The decision to add an investment product to an existing portfolio depends on the relative means and standard deviations of the investment vehicle and the existing portfolio as well as the correlation between the investment vehicle and the portfolio. The correlation between the S&P 500 and the CTA-based managed futures indices and sub-indices are between 0.15 and -.30.

As the managed Futures and Stocks and Bonds are negatively correlated, when they are combined in a portfolio, the risk levels are reduced and the returns are enhanced. Futures traders must note that the lowest level of return of the portfolio enhanced with zero and negatively correlated investments is about equal to the highest level of return for the traditional portfolio without investments in futures. The same goes for the risk factor.

The reason why the returns of public commodity funds have a low correlation with traditional investment vehicles such as stocks and bonds is the investment strategy applied by them. The stock and bond funds invest primarily in cash markets, whereas managed futures funds are restricted to futures and options markets.

Moreover, while the correlation between managed futures products and stock and bond portfolios is approximately zero, recent research has shown that when returns are segmented according to whether the stock/bond market rose or fell, managed futures are shown to have a negative correlation when these cash markets portfolios posted significant negative returns and are positively correlated when these cash portfolios reported significant positive returns. Thus managed futures may also offer unique asset allocation properties in differing market environments.

Managed Futures Trading and Futures Price Volatility

With all the above-discussed features, futures markets play a key role in modern market economies. It has certainly proven its worth; widely used for risk-shifting purposes by firms as varied as commodity merchants, investment banks, and pension funds. Formation of price expectations, production plans, and consumption schedules are also not unaffected by the futures prices.

The increase and decrease of futures prices depends on innumerable factors that may influence buyers' and sellers' judgments. Judgments about what a particular commodity will be worth at a given time in the future. The continuous process of the occurrence of latest development in the market followed by latest information available, allows reassessment of these judgments that affects the price of a particular futures contract. Futures trading thus require not only the necessary financial resources but also the necessary financial and emotional temperament.

It is considered that managed futures trading increases price volatility in these markets. For example, if large managed pools attempt to simultaneously buy futures contracts in the same market, futures prices may overshoot equilibrium values, and vice versa. In such situations, social welfare losses may result because incorrect futures price signals are sent to producers and consumers. Despite the importance of the issue, evidence regarding the impact of managed futures trading on futures price behavior is quite limited.

The determination of price is an important aspect of Futures Market. If prices are not discovered correctly, incorrect price signals will be communicated to producers and consumers. This will result in either a shortage or surplus of output and a loss in economic welfare.

Given the economic importance of futures markets, the efficiency of price discovery in these markets is very significant.

Economic Basis for Managed Futures Returns

While futures markets provide economic benefits to the underlying users of their markets, traders in futures markets are often viewed as operating in a zero sum game. However, the existence of a zero sum game does not restrict CTA's from obtaining superior risk and return tradeoffs relative to the assets.

Arbitrage profits and risk/return positions that replicate the underlying cash markets are potential benefits of managed futures. How?

CTAs can create futures positions similar if not identical investment positions to the deliverable cash instruments. Given the lower transaction costs of trading in futures markets, these cash position returns may be superior to the returns of underlying cash markets for comparable long positions. Also, institutional characteristics and differential carry costs among investors may permit CTAs to take advantage of short-term pricing differences between identical futures and cash market positions. Thus in contrast to a large number of traditional security traders, CTAs have opportunities that may generate profits under varying market conditions.

Additionally, speculative positions that are required as a means of meeting the demands of cash market participants may create investment situations were investors are required to offer speculators a 'risk' premium for holding open long (short) positions even in a world of arbitrage traders. This positive return to holding open futures may result positive rates of return in the underlying futures and options markets. This return to traders for offering liquidity and limiting losses may exist not only in futures markets but may exist in a wide range of derivative products.

Lastly, due to institutional factors such as, end of month processes, portfolio rebalancing, specialist risk positions, government actions, markets may trend for varying time periods in various markets. Low transaction costs combined with the ability to go short may permit the use of technical trading rules by managed futures to obtain positive returns in markets which, for short time periods, may be overvalued. In fact, these market cycles, embedded in cash market trading styles, have been used to explain some portion of the return to a technically based commodity futures trading system.

Conclusion

The stock markets in the U.S are moving towards the first consecutive three-year decline in 60 years. The disappointing equity returns and current economic environment is believed favorable for CTAs as investors are drawing their attention towards Managed Futures. Several bigger exchanges have reported all-time volume records in the recent months and the global trading volumes on futures are on their way to another record year in 2003. This is because CTAs often perform well during times of instability and uncertainty. Now is such a time, and these managers can potentially benefit from the present conditions.

The risk-return and correlation properties have already given a clear indication of the benefits of Managed Futures in a generic traditional portfolio. The ability of Managed Futures to offer a potential protection in periods when the stock markets are not performing well is one of its key strengths. This is the most important and valuable contribution and is the main factor that attracts institutional investors. Investors should consider having an exposure to this asset class.

In today's weird and uncertain political and economical climate it is prudent and wise to have Multiple Sources of Income. It is logical and self-explaining. You do not place all your *"income eggs"* in one basket. It is ideal to have a scenario suck as this below;

1. Work for a steady paycheck
2. Help others
3. Spread trader/broker

I choose to write and communicate as a vehicle of self-expression. It is my media. I often wish I chose painting or some other vehicle, as I am not a natural born storyteller. I could never write fiction.

Commodities will offer a better return and more interesting speculative opportunities in the coming decades according to Jim Rogers's ex-partner of George Soros. He believes in commodities so much that he started a commodities index fund. Currently he enjoys a 150-percent return on the fund. I have a course to teach you spread trading on futures

Obviously you need to learn about these businesses before you jump right in.
The main US futures markets are in Chicago, Ill and New York City. In addition to the main markets there are exchanges in Kansas City and Minneapolis as well.

Contracts

New futures contracts are established by the exchange after they petition it with the CFTC, upon approval the market can experiment and trade a standard contract that the exchange came up with. The older, more established contracts are:

Grains

   Corn

   Soybeans

   Wheat

Meats

   Pork Bellies

   Live Pork

   Live Cattle and so on (please see the major contract specifications in Appendix B)

The contract has size, delivery specification and price quote specifications. For example Corn is deliverable in 5000 bushels that is equal 1 contract. The grade of delivery is:

No. 2 Yellow at par, No. 1 yellow at 1 1/2 cents per bushel over contract price, No. 3 yellow at 1 1/2 cents per bushel under contract price

This means that Corn has three grades and some grades can be substituted for the other if paid a premium.

So when you see a quote for Corn like 203 ¼ this means 2 dollars and 3 ¼ cents expressed in cents only.

Futures contracts are not made equal and the volatility and total contract size is represented by the margins the exchange requires to be put down.

Players

Who are the people participating in the markets? There are two classes of players

The Hedgers sometimes also referred as Commercials and the Speculators who risk their funds in order to make profit.

Hedgers (or Commercials)

These are processors, grain companies who deal in the cash commodity. In order to hedge market risk they will speculate in the futures market with the opposite direction as their cash position may be.

So a grain processor who will receive cash (real) grain in its silos in three months time will pay the forward cash price even so he signed a contract today. In order to hedge his position he will buy grain futures because the rise in grain prices is what he is afraid of.

A grain merchant on the other hand perhaps has its own farm land. He is afraid of the prices falling for the harvest so he will place a short position and unwind it at harvest time.

If the grain prices indeed fall he will profit from the futures position that will be offset by the loss he will incur in the cash market. Should the prices rise he will gain in the cash market and lose in the futures. Of course the magnitude of the moves is not equal so he may gain or lose a little but for the most part he is protected. This arbitrage is the Risk Management using the futures markets.

Daily limits in Price movements

Since futures markets can get emotional and hectic adverse swings in prices can and do occur. In order to instill calm and rationale into the price action the exchanges restrict daily price movements. Since the markets are affected by events happening on weekends and 24 hours a day but traders can only participate during market hour's openings can occur with price gaps. When the limit for the daily range has been reached trading will cease until the market moves away from the limit or the trading hours come to the end.

The limits of each contract are posted on the website of the exchange and your broker can provide you with this information too. For example at the Chicago Board of Trade, Corn has a daily Limit of 20 cents/bu ($1,000/contract), none for spot month.

This means the most current month can move with no price restriction.

Ticks

Tick is a smallest unit a futures contract can fluctuate. As we show in this course – 1 tick for Corn is ¼ cent ($12.50). Since each commodity is different in total size each tick has different value.

Pit traded futures versus electronic markets

Traditionally commodities were traded in the pit. To some extent this is true even today. The active Eurodollar, US Treasury Bond and most **full-size** contracts are still pit traded, meaning the there is an open outcry and one on one human activity is involved with executing your trade.

Traditionally Chicago markets are open outcry - this means that orders are phoned in to the exchange and received by the floor clerk, and then a runner will take this order into the Pit and hands it to the broker. Of course nowadays, electronic hand held calculators and some technology exists. Orders are also flashed into the pit from the side where the clerks sort them out. Small orders have a way to be ignored in this hectic and archaic system. Critics of the exchanges have for a long time been critical of this system. Mistakes or so-called **out trades** occur. Fortunately the exchanges are *forced* by the competition to adopt and change. Eurex the European Futures exchange has opened an office in the US. They have al electronic order matching. Singapore trades Eurodollar contracts and since many bigger traders can rout their orders to Singapore the Chicago exchanges must slowly change and come into the 21st Century.

Electronic trading is good for the small trader and the one lot operator. This much is clear. **Globex** the electronic futures market is jointly owned by the CME and CBOT. It is a great venue for the new trader learning to trade today. It is the futures while open outcry is the pass.

When looking to trade a contract first you should examine the volume and volatility. Also the spread must be looked at.

The spread

The spread is the amount of **ticks** between the **bids** and **asked prices.** Imagine the market like this.

Corn bid at 224 ¼ *bid* – 224 ½ *asked* this means that the trader who is the **market maker** will sell Corn for 224 ½ - the *asked price* and he is willing to buy at ¼ the *bid price*.

On the floor and sometimes even off the floor they will abbreviate and use the last digit only so the quote for the market becomes Corn at 4 ¼ to 4 ½.

The market maker or scalper makes his living from the spread. If you put in an order to buy Corn at 4 ¼ he/she will only sell to you when the whole market has already moved to 4 bid – 4 ¼ offered on the floor. In some markets you can actually bid yourself and offer so effective you can be a market maker but often no one will trade with you unless the market has drifted already.

Bar

The bar in the bar hart can represent one minute or one hour.

```
      high
       ├ last
       │
       │
open ──┤
       │
      low
```

Choppy: intraday volatility > interday volatility

It is understood that constant calculation and number crunching may not be in your plans so there are other more subjective methods.

Look and see a specific chart. Picture is worth a thousand words.

1. Trends are chart and Market specific

2. Price and Confirmed with Momentum Oscillation determine trends

3. Markets are ALWAYS trending, sometimes in wide ranges and sometimes in tight ranges

4. Price creates Trends inside Trends or Minor Trends inside Extreme Trends.

5. Minor Trends Confirm Extreme Trends.

Number 3 is true but often you do not see these micro trends if only looking at end-of-day data.

Slippage

Slippage typically occurs in wild markets when **resting orders** become **market orders**. Imagine the scenario - most scared money traders will place close stops and pretty much everyone knows about these. So the big money non-scarred traders will try to push the market, and activity often described as **fishing for the stops.** The floor traders mainly do this activity and any new trader should be aware of this before risking a cent.

Daily Price Limits

Exchanges establish daily price limits for trading in futures contracts. The limits are stated in terms of the previous day's closing price plus and minus so many cents or dollars per trading unit. Once a futures price has increased by its daily limit, there can be no trading at any higher price until the next day of trading. On the other hand, once a futures price has declined by its daily limit, there can be no trading at any lower price until the next day of trading. This event is a **limit-down** day.

So, if the daily limit for a particular grain is currently 10 cents a bushel and the previous day's settlement price was $3.00, there can not be trading during the current day at any price below $2.90 or above $3.10. The price is allowed to increase or decrease by the limit amount each day. This day is also referred as a **limit-up** day.

For some contracts, daily price limits are eliminated during the month in which the contract expires. Because prices can become particularly volatile during the expiration month (also called the "delivery" or "spot" month), persons lacking experience in futures trading may wish to liquidate their positions prior to that time. Or, at the very least, trade cautiously and with an understanding of the risks, which may be involved.

Daily price limits set by the exchanges are subject to change. They can, for example, be increased once the market price has increased or decreased by the existing limit for a given number of successive days. Because of daily price limits, there may be occasions when it is not possible to liquidate an existing futures position at will. In this event, possible alternative strategies should be discussed with a broker.

Position Limits

Although the average trader is unlikely to ever approach them, exchanges and the CFTC establish limits on the maximum speculative position that any one person can have at one time in any one futures contract.

The purpose is to prevent one buyer or seller from being able to exert undue influence on the price in either the establishment or liquidation of positions – in plain English it prevents **cornering the markets**. Position limits are stated in number of contracts or total units of the commodity.

The easiest way to obtain the types of information just discussed is to ask your broker or other advisor to provide you with a copy of the contract specifications for the specific futures contracts you are thinking about trading. You can also obtain this information from the exchange where the contract is traded

Pivot Points

The pivot point is used as a predictive indicator. If the following day's market price falls below the pivot point, it may be then used as a new resistance level. Conversely, if the market price rises above the pivot point, it may act as the new support level.

There are several different methods for calculating pivot points, the most common of which is the five-point system. This system uses the previous days high, low and close, along with two support levels and two resistance levels (totaling five price points) to derive a pivot point.

The equations are as follows:

R2 = P + (H - L) = P + (R1 - S1)

R1 = (P x 2) - L

P = (H + L + C) / 3

S1 = (P x 2) - H

S2 = P - (H - L) = P - (R1 - S1)

Here, "S" represents the support levels, "R" represents the resistance levels, and "P" represents the pivot point. High, low and close are represented by the "H," "L" and "C," respectively.

R2 - 55.49

R1 - 54.56

P - 53.03

S1 - 52.10

S2 - 50.57

Order Entry 101

The need to communicate your intentions to buy or sell a futures contract is of some importance.
You can either use an electronic order platform or use the order desk of your broker to communicate your actions for the marketplace.

Market Orders

The simplest order is sometimes the least used. This is a market order
It communicates the floor or the electronic marketplace your wishes to buy or sell a number of futures contracts for the going market price. This is the bid and asked price for the contract in question. The order would go as it follows:

Corn Market – Dec Corn bid 234 ¼ - asked 234 ¾ - this would mean that as the buyer of 1 Dec Corn would pay 234 ¾
 If you were a seller of Corn the market would fetch 234 ¼ for your contract. There is some controversy on using Market orders in pit traded (old style). I will get to this in detail…

Limit Orders

These orders are also called *Resting orders*. Traders use these when they pick the price and wait for the market to come to them instead of stepping up to the plate and follow the crowd.

Stop Orders

These orders execute when and only *when* the market price trades "through" the stop price.

The **buy stop** must be placed **above** the market price to be even accepted by the floor or the order entry system.

This type of order can be used for two purposes:
- To establish a long position
- To get out of a short position that can turn out to be a loser (*protective stop*)

The later type of order is also called a **stop loss order**. Floor clerks sometime accept them but it is always good to use the proper terminology and avoid confusion. Floors are noisy and hectic at times. Since the order can be entered as an initial position the name is **Stop Order.**

The key is that these orders turn into a **market order** once they get triggered.

How do stop orders get triggered?

The ***buy stop*** gets triggered when and if the **market trades or is bid at or above** the stop price.

The ***sell stop*** gets triggered when and if the **market trades or is offered at or below** the stop price.

Market-if-touched orders (MIT)

These orders are also called ***board orders*** and they are similar to stop order in two ways;
1. The activation occurs when the price levels reach a certain point.
2. They become market orders once they are activated.

They are used differently from the Stop orders in a way they are placed.

A **buy MIT** order is placed **below** the current market price, and it will establish a long position or close a short position.

The **sell MIT** order is placed **above** the current market price, and it will establish a short position or close a long position.

How so these orders differ? Essentially the trade will use the appropriate order depending his/hers current position (if he/she flat or has no open position) or currently in the market.

You can see that the MIT can never be used to limit or "stop" losses incurring but the **stop order** can.

To enter the market at a certain point one can use either order with the notable differences. Traders who trade anticipating changes in the short term trend use MIT orders to in a sense draw the line for a support or resistance of a given price action. The **stop order** will work of you want to jump on a wave and see a move (either up or down) and want to come on board and surf that move. Since the buy stop is above the current market – initial position can be established of a certain resistance level is broken to the upside and it is perceived to safe buy since the price action is considered a **breakout.**

Do you see the subtle difference in the philosophy of trading? We shall get into this later too when we discuss trading styles.

Studying order process and appropriate techniques is the start for any beginner.

Establishing a **methodology** can never start too soon. Even if you never traded a single futures contract you should ask yourself "what type of a trader will I be"? Can I anticipate and predict or I will look at facts of price action and act accordingly. Neither is right or wrong but one or the other will suit your personality. It is hard but not impossible to change. My experience with traders shows that ones with the later philosophy trade for a little longer time frame and the traders who want to predict are the day-traders and **scalpers**. There are success stories in both camps.

MOO - Market on Open

This is an order to exit or enter the trades on the first 5 minutes of the trading day.

MOC – Market on Close

This is an order to exit or enter the trades on the last 5 minutes of the trading day

Stops or No Stops

This is the million-dollar question bugging many novice traders and even experienced futures operators.

The problem with tight stops is that the floor or the professional market maker crowd will 'gun' for these stops and try to trigger them and then reverse. This phenomenon is as old as the hills. The danger of **not using stops** is when the market is not just fishing for stops but genuinely reversed and going the other way and you are holding the bag. This is a recipe for losing in the futures markets.

Many larger professional traders use only mental stops and look at volume and other price action to gauge if the floor is truly moving the price or only fishing for stops. Further larger and more seasoned traders place their stops further away from the less savvy and *weaker hands*.

Orders have priority (highest to lowest) in the following sequence;

Market, Stop, MIT, Limit

Quiz - Market Order

A sell stop order at 8 becomes a market order if/when the commodity is

A) Offered at 8 or below

B) Bid at 8 or below

C) Offered at 8 or above

D) Bid or 8 and above

Charting and Indicators

Prediction

Prediction of future events is an ancient human wish. Apocryphal saying states: "it is difficult to make predictions, especially about the future".
However, the desire to make predictions remains as strong as ever, and is an important part of almost every aspect of human life.
The predictive indicators are for example used to be able to make trading decisions and use such indicator to "predict" price movement. Historical evidence shows that such indicators are far more unreliable and less in numbers than one would imagine.

Reaction

A reversal of the prevailing trend in price movement for a security. The term is most often used to describe a decline after a period of rising prices. A reaction is often considered beneficial for the long-term health of the market, in that the prices had risen too quickly and the drop put them back to more realistic levels. It is also called correction. When this price action is already observed it can be acted upon with some assurance and certainty that it will yield profit.

Price

Technical analysis in trading is based on price. This is because the price of a commodity at a given point are dependent on factors such as, the supply, the demand, the general economic outlook, the political climate, the optimism or the pessimism of the population etc. Price is considered to be a reliable indicator because it encompasses all these factors. So, when the price of gold increases indicators that buying (demand) has increased. The trading mantra is as long as the price goes up, stay with the trade.

Longer-term position traders trade all the markets; they consider all markets are the same because of the price factor. In this trading system markets are measured, compared and studied by their individual price movements. Therefore, position traders do not require understanding the trading markets; he only requires taking the price data and applying the rules.

Types of Indicators

Leading Indicators

Leading indicators are designed to lead price movements. Most represent a form of price momentum over a fixed period (both long and short term), which is the number of periods used to calculate the indicator.

Lagging Indicators

The trend traders use lagging indicators. Lagging indicators follow the price action and are commonly referred to as trend following indicators. They work best when markets or securities develop strong trends and are designed to keep the traders in the trade as long as the trend is intact. Some popular Trend following indicators includes moving averages and MACD. We are going to discuss these indicators here.

Moving Averages

Moving average presents data series in a way that identifies the direction of the trend. Moving averages do not predict a change in trend, but rather follow behind the current trend. MA's are calculated using 2 different methods:

By finding the average price of a security over a set number of periods.

An exponential moving average weighs more on recent prices relative to older prices. The shorter the exponential moving average is, the more weight that will be applied to the most recent price.

EMA = [C * K] + [yesterday's EMA (P)]* (1-K)]

Where K = 2/(1+N)

N = Number of periods for EMA

When the Price (C) is higher than yesterday's EMA (P), then the difference is positive (C - P). The positive difference is weighted by multiplying it by the constant ((C - P) x K) and the answer is added to the previous period's EMA, resulting in a new EMA that is higher ((C - P) x K) + P.

Similarly, when the current price is lower than the previous period's EMA, the difference will be negative (C - P). The negative difference is weighted by multiplying it by the constant ((C - P) x K) and the final result is added to the previous period's EMA, resulting in a new EMA that is lower ((C - P) x K) + P.

Moving averages identify and confirm trend, identify support and resistance levels, and develop trading systems. Moving averages helps to ensure that a trader is in line with the current trend. Once in a trend, moving averages keeps the trader in, but may also give late signals.

Rate of Change (ROC) and Momentum (MOM)

Momentum divides today's price by the price N days/weeks ago, calculated as: Cw - Cw N days ago

ROC subtracts today's price from a price N days/weeks ago, calculated as: Cw / Cw X days ago

(Cw is a MA of closing prices)

We know that an up trend is established when a security forms a series of higher highs and higher lows. A downtrend is established when a security forms a series of lower lows and lower highs. A trading range is established when a security neither establishes an up trend nor downtrend.

Traders could buy when an MA turns up in a downtrend and when a short MA crosses above a long MA. They should sell when MA turns down in an up trend and when a short MA crosses below a long MA.

Moving Average Convergence-Divergence (MACD)

The name of the indicator is implies that the shorter EMA continually converges toward and diverges away from the longer EMA.

MACD measures the difference between two moving averages. 12-day and 26-day MA's are common values for the short and long MA respectively. A positive MACD indicates that the 12-day EMA is trading above the 26-day EMA. If MACD is positive and rising, then the rate-of-change of the faster moving average is higher than the rate-of-change for the slower moving average. An increase in positive momentum is considered to be bullish. Similarly, a negative MACD is considered to be bearish. There are 3 common methods to interpret the MACD:

Crossovers - When the MACD falls below the signal line it is a signal to sell. It is vice versa - when the MACD rises above the signal line.

Divergence - When the security diverges from the MACD it signals the end of the current trend.

Overbought/Oversold - When the MACD rises dramatically (shorter moving average pulling away from longer term moving average) it is a signal the security is overbought and will soon return to normal levels.

Traders should buy when MACD turns up when < 0 and in a down trend and when MACD crosses above zero. They should sell when MACD turns down when > 0 and in an up trend and when MACD crosses below zero.

Channels (or Bands)

These indicators determine trend boundaries. Creating an upper and lower boundary that encloses all the points on the chart does this. Traders close the position when the price turns down at or near the upper line. Similarly, in a downtrend, trader would go short when the price turns down on or near the MA line. They set a stop on or one point above the last high at entry and close the position when the price turns up at or near the lower line.

One famous band is the *Bollinger Band*

Williams %R

Williams %R is used to determine market entry and exit points. A Williams reading over 80% usually indicates a stock is oversold while readings below 20% is considered overbought.

Williams %R is plotted as a single line and is calculated like this:
Williams %R = (Hw - Close / Hw - Lw) * 100

Hw = highest close for a time window determined by the trader and Lw is the lowest close for the same time window.

Traders could buy when Williams %R fails to reach the lower reference line in a downtrend and turns up. They should sell when Williams %R fails to reach the upper reference line in an up trend and turns down.

Parabolic SAR

J. Welles Wilder Jr. developed the Parabolic SAR where **SAR** stands for *stop and reverse*.

A trade is signaled when the price bars and stop levels intersect:
- Go long when price meets the Parabolic SAR stop level, while short.
- Go short when price meets the Parabolic SAR stop level, while long.

Stochastic

In an upwardly trending market, prices tend to close near their high and during a downward trending market; prices tend to close near their low. The Stochastic Oscillator compares where a security's price closed relative to its price range over a given time period. These indicators are of two types: **fast and slow**. As the name suggest fast stochastic reacts quickly to price changes, is volatile and gives more bad signals than slow stochastic. This is the reason why most people prefer **slow stochastic**. These are displayed as two lines, the main line is "%K" and the second line is "%D" - moving average of %K.

Fast stochastic is calculated as:

%K = (Close - Lw / Hw - Lw) * 100

%D = %K smoothed with a 3 day MA

Where, Lw is the lowest close for a specific time window; Hw is the highest close for the same time window.

Slow stochastic is calculated as:

%K = %D from fast stochastic

%D = %D from fast stochastic smoothed again with a 3 day MA

%K and %D Recap

- %K (fast) = %K formula presented above using x periods
- %D (fast) = y-day SMA of %K (fast)
- %K (slow) = 3-day SMA of %K (fast)
- %D (slow) = y-day SMA of %K (slow)
- %K (full) = y-day SMA of %K (fast)
- %D (full) = z-day SMA of %K (full)

There is a third type the Full Stochastic.

The Full Stochastic uses three parameters: the period for %K (fast), the period for the SMA that smoothes %K (fast), and the period of the SMA that forms %D (full). While the tool provides some excellent default values we shall not examine it in detail.

Traders should buy when either %K or %D falls below a specific level (e.g., 20) and then rises above that level. They should sell when the %K line rises above the %D line and when the Oscillator rises above a specific level (e.g., 80) and then falls below that level (or if the %K line falls below the %D line.

Relative Strength Index (RSI)

RSI measures the ratio of up closings to down closings and ranges between 0 and 100. A popular method of analyzing the RSI is to look for a divergence in which the market index is making a new high, but the RSI is failing to surpass its previous high. This divergence is an indication of a reversal in the near future. RSI is calculated like this:

RSI = 100 - (100 / 1 + R/S)

R = an average of upward price change.

S = an average of downward price change.

Traders could buy when RSI breaks a down trend line and should sell when RSI breaks an up trend line.

Directional Movement Indicator (DMI)

DMI is one of the most complex indicators in technical analysis. It determines not only the trend of prices, but also the strength of the trend. When used with the up and down directional indicator values, +DI and -DI, the average directional movement index, or ADX, determines the market trend. A long position is established whenever the +DI crosses above the -DI. When the -DI crosses above the +DI, the long position is liquidated and a short position is established. When ADI is going up, the strength of the trend is growing and indicates a more powerful trend and vice-versa.

Traders could buy when +DI is above -DI and ADX is rising and sell when sell when +DI is above -DI and ADX is falling.

Elder-ray (ER)

ER measures the upward and downward pressure on prices. In up trends the upward pressure on the MA will be greater than the downward pressure and vice versa. It uses a combination of the current trend to give a signal. ER is calculated like this:

- Calculate an MA of closing price
- Up pressure = High - EMA
- Down pressure = Low - EMA

Traders should buy when the trend is up, when the down pressure is rising but still negative. They should sell when the trend is down and up pressure is rising but still positive.

Volatility

This indicator is mainly used for option evaluation.

The key to using historic volatility is determining the correct period of time for each market. The market you are looking at may show a history of volatility years ago but may have been relatively calm the last few months. Getting an idea of the markets behavior recently may be of no use to the trader that is looking at distant options and vice versa for the trader looking at near term options.

Volume

Volume is also one of the basic measures of trading activity. Defined as the number of shares that changed hands in a given period of time, Volume measures investor interest in a stock. It is considered that volume is based on the price of a trade. Technical analysis in trading couples price and volume: when prices move sharply, volume should also be high. Volume indicators create a running total of volume by adding or subtracting a portion of a day's/week's volume based on how the stock performed during that duration. On-balance Volume (OBV), Accumulation-Distribution, and Force Index are all volume indicators. We have a special section on volume and open interest.

On-Balance Volume (OBV), Accumulation-Distribution (AD), and Force Index (FI)

OBV, AD, and FI are all volume-based indicators that confirm or deny trends based on volume. Trading signals are generated when these indicators diverge (move opposite) the trend.

On-Balance Volume (OBV)

OBV measures positive and negative volume flow. Based on the fact that volume precedes price, it calculates a running total of volume by adding a period's volume when the close is up and subtracting the period's volume when the close is down. Traders should buy when OBV breaks its trend line in a downtrend and sell when OBV breaks its trend line in an up trend.

Accumulation/Distribution

Accumulation/Distribution is similar to OBV but instead of adding the entire day's volume to the running total, it only adds or subtracts a portion of the volume based on the following formula:

A/D = (close - open / high - low) *

Traders should buy when AD diverges from a new price high and sell when AD diverges from a new price low. Track 'N Trade even helps with arrows pointing put the divergence.

FI

FI multiplies the day's volume by the difference between today's close and yesterday's close. The index increases with the gap.

FI = volume * (today's close - yesterday's close)

Traders should buy when FI drops below zero when price is in an up trend and sell when FI crosses above zero when price is a downtrend.
Market has no room for literal interpretation. The ability of the trader will be more defined by his/her visceral awareness of price dynamics within a trend or range as it compares to mathematical indications than by purely literal interpretation.

I have some studies in the Money management unit that trading involves some real mathematics. It isn't a holy grail in any sense. Technical analysis with trading acts like an X-ray machine that generates pictures of market conditions. For a trader to limit himself to technical analysis is like limiting to X-ray findings. For further treatment one has to get hold of other means of cures. Traders understand that there is no technical analysis that is a prerequisite to long term trading. The only thing that matters is the 'price'.

Successful trading is not based on Fibonacci numbers, the golden mean, nor is it related to the works of Gann or Elliott. Predictive indicators such as, Gann, Fibonacci, moving average stochastic, MACD, Bollinger, Williams, RSI or ADX, are sometimes depended too heavily and are not overly used by very successful traders. As we have studied earlier in this section that these indicators are all designed to predict what a market would do. *Successful traders know the predictive limitations of mortal humans.*

Technical indicators are good for studying and have place in the market, but *trading masters* do not fixate on indicators. The role of technical indicators in a long-term Position Trading system is just as a part of a complete reactive trading system. The only true method for trading is a long-term Position Trading system that reacts to the market.

When trading like a true *master* knowing the exact odds of any one trade isn't as important as knowing whether or not the trade has a positive expectancy. One cannot always accurately predict which way a market will move or how far it will go but trading only with a positive expectancy he should win over time.

Seasonal Trends and Geopolitics 101

Paying attention to government reports, their analysis and pundits paid or self-appointed has limitations. It is hard to follow 15 major futures markets. Market analysis and news in geopolitics and world events have use for the trader but information must be used carefully and only after careful scrutiny.

Fundamental news and reports are usually priced into the markets and therefore have serious limits. If anything their contrarian value should be emphasized.

Commitment of Trader's Report

The one exception to this is Commitment of Trader's Report. Let us find out what this actually means.

The exchanges require position reporting for their members and outside customers. This data is then compiled and reported by the CFTC. The reports are broken down to small traders and large traders and they reflect positions. This fundamental data is essentially the inside information of the futures industry. I hope you realize the value of such data.

The only diminishing aspect of this report is of course that everyone has access to this. Common access does not mean universal understanding. The reason is again trading style. Very short-term traders often do not have the time and inclination to pay attention to every nuance of their respective markets. Gecko Software has a plug-in for the COT data and they distribute it with Track 'N Trade Pro.

As you see the graphs shows the level of large traders and hedgers versus the small trades. Track 'N Trade will even "interpret" the data and provide signals. The signals are correct as you can see but not always present. It is advisable to use the COT information in conjunction with other indicators. What separates the COT signal from the rest? It is based on fundamental information and position of other well-informed market participants and hedgers. Who are the hedgers of Gold? Large Jewelry processors, gold mines and electronics companies who use large amount of gold are all hedgers. Do you think they would have in depth knowledge of gold markets and the prognosis for the near future? You bet they do. Commitment of Traders Report is very powerful tools for the individual trader.

Just looking back to this last move in Crude oil to the upside from around $40/barrel (on July 29 2004) to $48 (on Aug 3, 2004) would be a gain of $7600 on just one Crude contract. Will this always work? I do not know. The reason I am demonstrating this to you here is to get your attention. You will also see that you did not have to take a position as the first. Early bird gets the biggest worm but the cat is still out in the dark mornings so be aware of this. The danger is always bigger at the turn of the market. Risk and reward would indicate that of course being first you would have made almost $12000 on one full-sized contract. But do you see how this market looks? Scary, in my opinion…

The Williams %R has turned positive and gave us a buy signal. It would have taken huge "cahones" to take this trade. Most big traders expect the market take out the most recent highs that acts as near term resistance level. And of course this is exactly as happened. I know you will say hindsight is 20/20 vision but I am just trying to make a point.
The COT indicator acted when the large traders stepped in. You will not likely to go broke coat tailing the Big Boys.

Geopolitics

Good traders have the thirst for knowledge and are curious as cats by nature. It is clear that we sometime are not privy to information that moves prices only months sometimes years later we hear the real news behind a major move. It is hard to get the right information at the right time.
Having said this one also cannot live in isolation and ignore what's going on. Despite what I hear of hermits trading only on prices I would have top believe that they have CNN at least. Since the CIA allegedly gets their information from CNN you should be on equal footing.

I tell you what I read day in day out. It is the Economist. I like to hang out at Borders or some bookstore and go through the Economist, I do not even buy them I just have my coffee and spend an hour or so sometimes less.
Futures traders need to know what's going on at least at the Macro level. You need to have a perspective, a picture of currency markets and commodities like gold or crude oil.
Do not ever let this "macro view" cloud your market acumen and timing.

The Internet is also the source of a wealth of information and data. Actually there is overkill there and one must be careful what to read there are so many sources, many outright incorrect.

Futures Calendars

USDA and various agricultural, energy agencies report on the state of the crops, reserve stocks and export import balances. Overseas supply and demand statistics are also reported. The importance of having a calendar is not that you wish to predict or take positions based on the news but the fact that news will invariably move the markets. Often it is not towards the direction one would expect.

Scanning for trades

Once you know what type of trading you want to do and what setup are you looking for – in theory the rest should come easy. In practice however you have over 45 futures to choose from.

In comparison the futures market is still better than the stock market where you have over 5000 stocks to find the one you trade.

Some traders use newsletters or web sites to pre-scan the markets and after a handful of candidates already selected – they go to work.

When learning to trade one can forgo the trade selection and go right to the tradecraft of trading the grains on paper first. Picking the grains for just an example, in reality the beginner can select any group of commodities and paper-trade them using Track 'N Trade.

Psychology

As I have alluded to this before, it is always a prudent and wise choice to ask - "why I am trading". Do you trade because you hate your job? Or is it because you are bored and need some diversion?

Asking these questions and asking them **early** can be of a huge help to get you started on the right mode. Whatever your motivation is the end result comes down to your result at the year end when you and your accountant sits down and sorts out what to report the IRS. Ideally your motive should be **money** and money **only**. As you are in a business – a trading business you can only measure your success, one way – with your account size.

Ed Seykota, the legendary futures trader said this; "Everyone gets out of the market what they want and expect." I believe this secretly implies that some people have the psychological make up to lose and they trade with an already defeatist attitude. Do not let this happen to you. Examine and always be in check with your mood, circumstance in life and finally your expectation of yourself. One good example is the trader who has the urge to be right all the time.

When facing a loss many traders will look at the market with a cold, calculated notion and knowing the conditions are not optimal to trade quit for the day. Traders who decide to "make the money back" often lose more than the original loss was. Why? Because of their frame of mind is not optimal at that point. Trading right you will need two conditions to work in harmony…

- Your own mind and psychology AND
- The market conditions

…Will have to exist in order to risk money and win.

Getting even with the market or compounding problems when feeling anger, anxiety over losses is not a right frame of mind to trade in. This is a **compulsive behavior**.

Certain core psychology and mental condition can exist in the trader to slow progress and hinder their efforts to become profitable. It is easier to trade if you have an even and calm personality that lacks compulsive behavior and can use self-control.

One can overcome these problems two ways.

One is NLP or Neuro-Linguistic Programming. This is a behavioral modification technique that sometimes helps speculators control bad habits and negative thinking.

"NLP - the name sounds complex, yet it is purely descriptive. Neuro refers to our nervous system - the mental pathways our five senses take which allow us to see, hear, feel, taste and smell.

Linguistic refers to our language ability; how we put together words and phrases to express ourselves, as well as how our "silent language" of movement and gestures, our body language.

Programming, taken from computer science, refers to the idea that our thoughts, feelings and actions are like computer software programs. When we change those programs, just as when we change or upgrade software, we immediately get positive changes in our performance. We get immediate improvements in how we think, feel, act and live." - *Charles Faulkner of New Market Wizards*

NLP is about **state** management. We perform depending in the *state* we are in. Some also call that mental frame. NLP will make sure that when performing crucial tasks such as sports and trading one is in the best form possible. Others refer to NLP as self-hypnosis. No matter what you call it – empirical evidence show that it works.

One thing I do not believe in is giving up your dreams even if you suffer from some disorder.

Good rules to follow:
- Do not trade when upset or when going through life altering changes
- Do no trade when suffering from a series of losses that may affect your trading
- Do no not trade under the influence of any drug (legal or illegal) unless it is prescribed by a doctor

Understanding the problem and dealing with it is the first step to managing and controlling it.

You do not need to be suffering from any disorder just to lose money. Often situations of your own making can hinder your progress as a trader.

Trading with Scarred Money

This is a very typical problem with so many. Wanting to trade and have this great business but not having enough funds to start. Many people will deal with this as best they can – keep the day job and dabble into trading on the side. That is OK; if you trade with money you can afford to lose. Your personal saving habits should be adjusted and focus on **making money** should replace **spending money**.

Spending money from a trading account is not wise unless you need the money for your household. After making a good trade the last thing you should do is to buy a new car. Yet many people will do just that. This is also trading psychology. Spend and spend on credit is the American Way. I do not blame the people – after all they are bombarded with adverts and the example their government shows is the worst. They spend your grandkids future away.

Making money is easier if you have more of it. Spending your ammunition and bullets in a war for a wasting asset (a car) is not *right thinking*.

Think of trading as war. It is a **zero sum** game. In futures especially more than the stock market, for every winner there must be a loser. This is reality. Your mind should be adjusted to this. Dan Akroyd who played Charles Winthorp the III depicted the best way the "war" in the classic comical movie "Trading Places".

"You make no friends in the pits and you take no prisoners. One moment you're up half a mil in soybeans and the next, boom, your kids doesn't go to college and they've repossessed your Bentley."

Trading Size

Much of the danger and *ill* notions of futures markets come from lack of education and improper practices. Many neophyte traders will trade bigger than they should. Sometimes this comes from the general lack of good trading education sometimes it is **ego** and **pride.** Of course trading size is what we all aspire and want. Young males are full of Testosterone. Ego will be a major factor. Blowouts will happen.

As I have said it. Trading is *War*. The guy who blinks last will win. You can be on the right side of a blowout when egomaniacs trade or you can be the one who blows out. It is your choice. Trading a proper mindset is easier if you have a well-defined and well-tested methodology. Then all you need to do is to follow the plan. Do not second-guess it and do not abandon it too soon.

You cannot truly achieve large, consistent returns until you disassociate money and ego from your trading method. This means that you have to trade only to trade well. If you have a positive expectancy system and smart risk management, the profits will come on their own.

Boredom

Boredom, like any other negative emotion, is a misuse of the mind. Beginning traders work on changing the way you think and try eliminating boredom as it is a danger to your business and finances.

Many full time traders dread the waiting between set-ups and find that idle time very distracting. Learn to use that time well. Do not through away that free time to idle pastimes. Learn and plan ahead.

So far you have read my observations and I am not trained in psychology nor I understand other traders as some who spent years and talking and consulting with them.

This is what some of the experts say. This is an excerpt from an interview with Dr. Brett Steenbarger, one of the world's leading authorities on trading psychology.

"The first vice is perfectionism, the tendency to set unreasonable goals and standards for oneself. I can't tell you how often I've heard a trader express frustration with a winning trade because "I should have taken more out of the move." What the trader is really saying is, "I should have been able to catch the absolute highs and lows." Because their standard is unrealistic, it sets them up for frustration, turning winning trades into psychological failures. If traders find themselves using the term "should" frequently when talking about their trading, there's a good chance that perfectionism is lurking in the background. Perfectionism is not about being achievement oriented or competitive; perfectionism is a repetitive emotional pattern of self-talk that says, "What you've done isn't good enough.

The second vice is ego. Ego enters into our trading when we write a blank check for our self-esteem, allowing our feelings about ourselves to ride the ups and downs of our P/L statements. Hanging onto losing trades to avoid feeling like a loser: that's one manifestation of ego. Impulsively putting on a trade after a losing trade to make back your money—revenge trading--that's ego at work as well. One of the most common but subtle examples of ego is the tendency to fight the market by picking tops and bottoms. This leads traders to fade strong markets and buy falling ones. This can work fine in range-bound markets, but inevitably leads to disastrous drawdowns in trending markets. If the need to be right—to beat the market—is stronger than the need to make money, the seeds of trading self-destruction are sown.

The third vice is overconfidence. Traders often assert that their trading is hurt by a lack of confidence. My experience, however, is that it is more common for traders to be hurt by their overconfidence. A simple litmus test that distinguishes valid confidence from overconfidence is to keep a log of each trade placed during a day or week (or, better yet, videotape your trading) and ask the question: "What was my edge for this trade?" If you cannot identify a specific edge for the trade, the odds are good that your trade is born of overconfidence. Very often, overconfidence takes the form of overtrading: actively trading narrow, thin markets, trading position size that is inappropriate for one's account size. Overconfidence is also evident when traders focus on entries but fail to identify exits, particularly to stop losses. It is easier to think about entries—the opportunities to make money—than face the possibility of loss or limits on profits. Great traders have an understanding of—and respect for—risk management. When that respect is missing, overconfidence is generally the culprit.

We can conclude that Speculating will tax and challenge ones psyche enormously. Speculating is 90% mental. Any imbalance in ones thinking and character will be detrimental to his or her speculating success.

Meditation

Life, especially the life of a Speculator can be very stressful. Research shows that regular meditation can reduce and sometimes eliminate stress and the harmful heath effect of it. If this is a little too "new age" for the reader, there is an analogy that could help to perhaps open ones mind about meditation.

Western philosophy re labeled meditation with prayer.

While prayer does not usually work in managing bad trades or losing positions that one had failed to manage and control. Meditation can perhaps maintain ones inner balance and perspective on life.

IRA Accounts for Futures

Futures Trading in an IRA account is sometimes problematic. This comes from the limited custodial setups available in the US and the IRS's tendency of interpreting the rules on the fly. Further the custodial fees assessed by the Trust company can be expensive and incurred annually. One way to get around this is to trade futures with Interactive Broker and use their custodial for Roth IRA.

If you trade actively i.e. make frequent profitable trades in your futures IRA account, you may run afoul of certain IRS tax code, which says you are engaging in producing business income. And you run the risk of the IRS disqualifying the entire tax-free status of the account. Simply put, if you buy one futures contract and hold it for three months and it makes $200 profit while you go about your daily job, the IRS likely will leave you alone. But if you trade your $20,000 account aggressively into $750,000 by trading actively, they might just find a way to eliminate the tax-free status of your account.

The key word being "*might*". It seems like a total gray-area. Ask your attorney or tax professional first.
However note this - Tax accountants and lawyers who might know the most about this subject might have a vested interest in day-trading IRAs being a tax problem. Why? Because if there is no problem to frequently trade futures in an IRA, then the vast majority of people will just trade futures in their Roth IRA. Who cares about trader status, corporate entities (to write-off expenses) if you can trade 100% tax-free and keep your life simple? You can always have a separate regular trading account to write off your expenses anyway.

So the tax firms most familiar with trader tax laws might actually have a vested interest in scare mongering about this issue.

Gold

Richard Nixon has lifted the gold standard in 1973; ending fixed monetary currency convertibility, which meant that one-ounce of gold could be converted at 33 dollars. History of gold goes back much longer than the US dollar however in modern times it is hard to separate the two. During the time between 1933-1971 US citizens could not own gold. In fact the US was the only country where the government confiscated gold from its citizens.

It can be argued that the de-linking of the dollar and gold was inevitable. According to Tom Wheat in his book-online the "A State of Clear and Present Danger: *A History of American Foreign Policy during the Cold War*[2] - in 1965 foreign banks with overseas branches held assets in excess of 100 billion dollars.

Clearly they intended to have gold instead of paper money. Historically Europe had inflationary times where they carted currency in wheel barrels. They considered a stable currency a temporary phenomenon and later history showed them right.

By the early 1970's claims on the dollar had risen to 1 trillion dollars. The US had three expensive wars to fight during these years; the Vietnam War, the Cold War and the War on Poverty. Government spending skyrocketed; according to the Keynesian law of economics the US had only two options to either borrow money from private banks or to devalue the currency.

Monetary policy with Western Europe called to keep their currencies in parity with the dollar as well. Essentially the US managed to 'export' its cold war deficits to Europe. As these policies were artificial they naturally could only stall the economic contrition and the fall of the dollar.

By 1971 US gold stock in Fort Knox declined to 10 billion dollars. Foreign Banks at the same time held 80 billion dollars or 8 times the supply of US gold reserves.

---

[2] http://www.geocities.com/s011023/coldwar9.htm

In the same year the US signed the *Smithsonian Agreement* that provided monetary controls that prevented the dollar freefall resulting in gold claims. The US dollar however was devalued 10 percent.

What followed this period was high inflation and continued dollar instability brought forward by the continuing Vietnam War, OPEC embargo and uncontrolled government spending.

By 1980 gold and silver has reached unprecedented highs and the discount rate was at 21 percent.

Some scholars even advocate bringing back the gold standard. Roger W. Garrison in his Paper "The 'Cost' of a Gold Standard" examines and refutes some of the arguments against the gold standard that are chiefly based on cost. Garrison states that the assumed equivalence of monetary stability and price level stability does not account for the insatiable appetite of politicians to spend.

Interestingly the current fiscal situation is strangely similar to the 70's. After some years of surpluses, proceeding the burst of the Internet bubble and 9/11 government spending spirals out of control.

The climate during the "War on Terror" rendered any politician impotent who wanted to voice caution and fiscal prudence.

No politician will have any longevity in political life that will raise his or her voice against the spending on "War on Terror".

As the result the US deficit has more than doubled from 2002 to 2003 and the dollar naturally has fallen steadily against the Euro and the Yen.

US officials even made statements that construed 'talking down" the dollar. US exporters do benefit from the lower dollar and it is believed that increased exports and low interest rate rendered the US immune of the long-term effect of the fall of the dollar.

There are several problems with such theories. Any fall of a currency can be hard to stop, effect similar to an avalanche could manifest and events can snowball and get out of control.

Any country that loses control over its currency chances the loss of its sovereignty.

When people lose faith in the value of their currency they start storing wealth in the traditional safe heavens like antiques, land, gold and other tangibles.

A sizeable underground economy can flourish that is impossible to tax that leads further to the decline of the currency and the impotency of the government.

Currently the government controls inflation and the released statistics of several price indices. It is notable that the released figures often exclude food and energy, like those were luxuries and discountable from statistical reports.

One other cost that is excluded from the official inflation watching indices is healthcare costs. No wonder.

The average healthcare cost rose double digits in the last decades annually. I believe the real inflation is much higher than the government reports it. The true picture can be seen only if one compares purchasing power of one dollar in the seventies with the purchasing power of one dollar today (2003).

The price of gold is chiefly driven by supply and demand. As a commodity it bears the cost of production and storage. It is also an industrial commodity used primarily for production of jewelry, ornaments and in the semiconductor industries.

Gold prices started moving up during 9/11 and the aftermath where the stock markets were closed for a few days and fallen after their opened.
Most people suspected that these moves in gold were just a reaction to the unprecedented events taking place during 9/11. Contrarian thinkers were again rewarded; gold started a major bull market.

How much gold is in Fort Knox?

As most people are aware Fort Knox is the place where the US gold reserves are kept. Several theories and urban legends were floating about army trucks leaving Fort Knox and carrying with them the bulk of the gold kept in Fort Knox. I like to ignore and dismiss innuendoes and urban legends as baseless and hearsay.

However the facts regarding the gold reserves are not at all comforting. James Turk, the editor of "Freemarket – Gold and Money Report" has asked the US Treasury Secretary, Lawrence Summers about an audit in 1999.

After his request was ignored by Mr. Summers, Mr. Turk wrote a letter to John Sununu who then was a congressman. The congressman could not be ignored and Mr. Turk received a reply from the US Treasury. His conclusion based on the reply is that it appears that the gold is safely in Fort Knox. [3]

Warren Buffett Sr. on Gold

Everyone knows and respects Warren Buffett and his prowess about money. It is little know fact that what Mr. Buffett knows about money he had learned from his father, Mr. Buffett Sr. who had served as a representative in Congress in the late 1940's.

In 1948 the Honorable Sr. Buffett had addresses a group of businessmen.

His speech was published two days later in *The Commercial and Financial Chronicle*, and has been reprinted by the Committee for Monetary Research & Education (10004 Greenwood Court, Charlotte, NC 28215-9621), a not-for-profit organization dedicated to the restoration of sound money.

"Today Congress is constantly besieged by [special interest] groups seeking benefits from the public treasury. Congressmen find it difficult to persuade themselves not to give in to pressure groups. With no bad immediate consequence it becomes expedient to accede to a spending demand. The Treasury is seemingly inexhaustible. Besides the unorganized taxpayers back home may not notice this particular expenditure - and so it goes."

The following words ring true today, as they were true 45 years ago. The only way citizens can put their representatives in short leash if they can demand gold for the dollars they earn.

"Before 1933 the people themselves had an effective way to demand economy. Before 1933, whenever the people became disturbed over Federal spending, they could redeem their paper currency in gold, and wait for common sense to return to Washington."

"That happened on various occasions and conditions sometimes became strained, but nothing occurred like the ultimate consequences of paper money inflation."

"When the people's right to restrain public spending by demanding gold coin was taken away from them, the automatic flow of strength from the grass-roots to enforce economy in Washington was disconnected."

---

[3] http://www.fgmr.com/response.htm

In 1991, Mr. Buffett Jr. has purchased 130 million ounces of silver through his company the *Berkshire Hathaway.*

How can the average person take advantage of these trends?

Gold and silver can be purchased in the pure form as coinage and ingots bars. Storage consideration and essaying must be kept in mind if one considers owning metals in this form.

The other way is to own mining shares. Owning shares in the mining companies is not as pure as owning the metal itself but can be very rewarding if certain due diligence is kept in mind. The company must have good financial standing and should be a leader in its group whether it is gold, platinum, silver etc.

One could also invest in a hedge fund invested in the gold futures market — a fund that would use the leverage of futures to play on the anticipated rise in the gold price.

Will gold help you surviving in treacherous times?

You have two choices; be *poor* or be *rich* both will have *some* insulation from the coming calamities in the world financial markets.

It always helps to look in price relationships than prices themselves

Chart 1

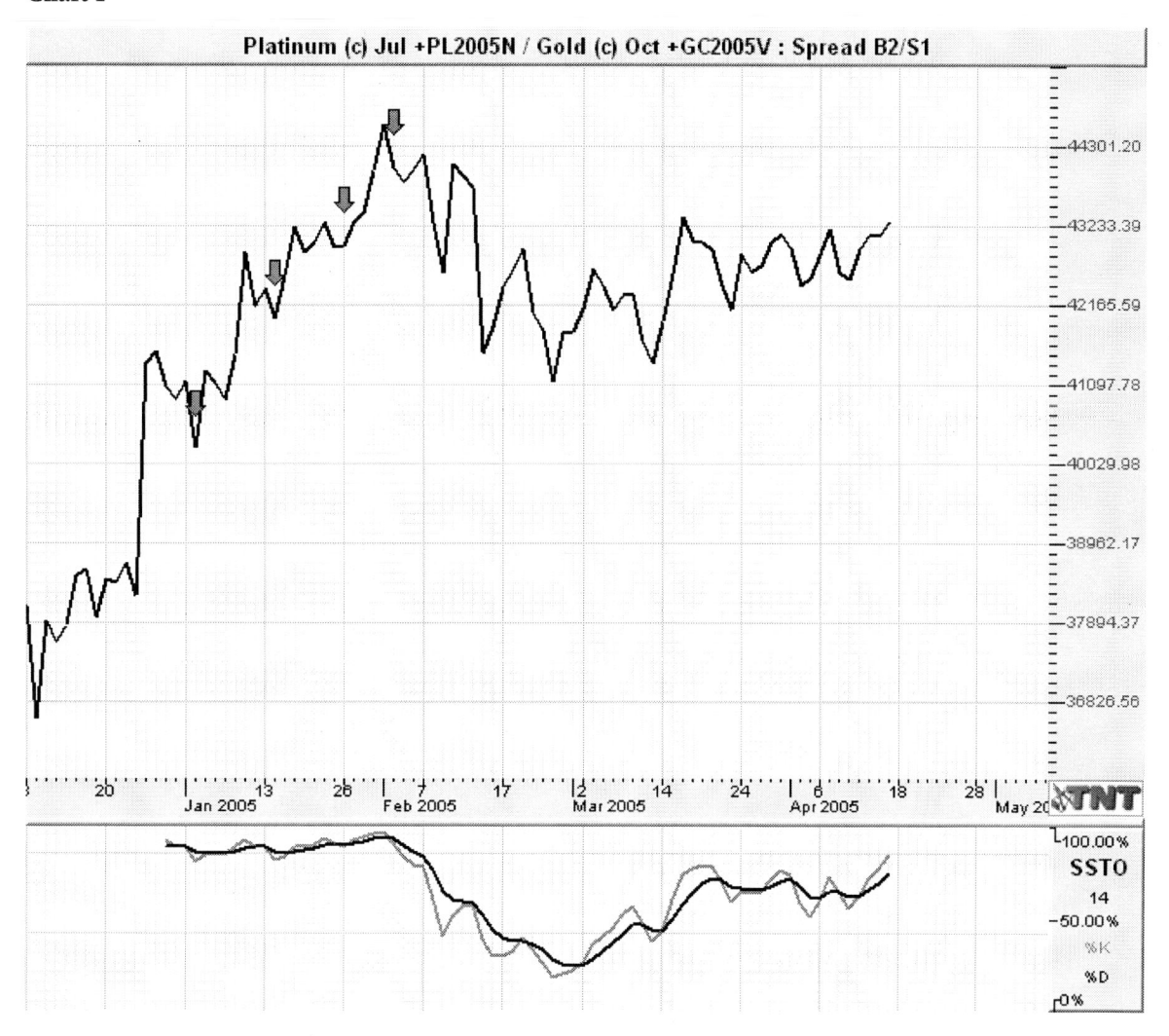

This is no different with Gold. Take for example the Platinum and Gold spread. (2x1) (See Chart 1).

Other good metals spreads are Gold versus Silver.

Uncertainty drives up Gold and Industrial use and offshore hoarding drives up Silver.

Being poor, while it is not all fun, is far better in the US than anywhere else in the world. We currently live in a practically socialistic welfare system where the masses are given free food and in many cases shelter too.

Neo-conservative Policymakers wish to change much of the current social safety net but I predict they will not succeed.

The Rodney King riots are ever etched in the memories of the politicians and policy makers. Imagine what would happen if the banks were to close and the public were again forbidden to own gold?

The American people are as generous as impatient in my observation. They do not trust their government and I predict this trust will be waning in the future as well.

Sadly it is the working middle class that takes the shaft and pays the burden.
In fact the middle class has been shrinking steadily since the 50's. In bad times the working middle class people are the endangered species. Since livable wages and decent work had been outsourced to India and China. Despite that legitimate business practices are largely replaced by Multi Level Marketing gimmicks and outright fraud, the self-employed can sometime escape the trap.

So you have decided you rather be rich than poor? In economic calamity typically the underground economy and the so-called *cash economy* grows as the rest of the system crumbles.

Montana ranches and real estate will always have value (I think). Gold coins or 18K chains will always buy you some food and services.

As a trader/investor learn to stash away your profits and do not blow it on fast women or beautiful horses (or the other way around...). Buy some rental property, some business, anything that could have lasting value.

During the last hyperinflation in Europe the self-employed people found survival somewhat easier. They simply worked for gold chain pieces instead of useless currency. As people still need plumbing and services this had worked to some extent.

Traders and speculators will survive if they are right about the trends they are betting on.

I don't mean to alarm you or steer you wrong. Honestly I do not know what exactly will happen and when.

Actually I consider myself an optimist because while I believe these events as inevitable I also think it will be over fast. Those who think change is not possible with the two party system stalemate we are having I suggest you remember to the Fall if the Soviet Union.

When you expect things to unfold you can prepare better and manage these evens to your advantage. When we stumble it is always a good idea to quickly sit down first.

Brokers

Love them or hate them unless you are a floor trader you cannot speculate with out an account with a broker. Brokers can and do many things for you. Do research, write newsletters, and provide you trading software and advice. Hold your hands while you are going through hard–times and more.

How much of this service you need it is entirely up to you.

If you trade spread however *smart* broker selection is not a bad idea. Human interaction and order analysis is more important with spreads than trading futures outright.

Nowadays we have software to enter spreads but some traders are not too trusting to software either.

Ultimately what cost structure you choose will depend on the style of trading and amount of contracts you trade in a day. If you are a day-trader you do need to watch your commissions indeed. Frequency of trading is the key.

The other factor is the stops you use. Some active traders do not use stops at all they watch the markets and they only have 'mental stops' usually in a form of an alert or signal.

What I am saying is once you have a position your trading frequency may not be entirely up to you.

Brokers who offer a system in a form of a newsletter or email alert want to be compensated for that service. Some newsletters are sold independently some are provided by the broker.

Where are the customer's yachts?

I remember this book - a very cynical piece suggesting that brokers have Yacht so should the customers. First of, not all brokers make the trading choices for the customers. That is called *discretionary trading.* More often brokers will make recommendations, send out newsletters and offer advice and service and not make the calls on buy or sell. The risk and the reward of the trade are born by the client. If the broker is making a lot of money *could* because he/she maybe offering exceptional service and has many clients.

Broker selection should be viewed as a precarious and delicate matter. If you want the cheapest commission you will get that and no service. You cannot expect both. However it is ultimately your choice and will have to match your trading style.

Technology is not everything

Computers and software are tools; ultimately it will not determine your success or failure as a trader. Brokers discount or full service will not have the ultimate say whether you are going to make it in this business or not. What is important that your choices will reflect your personality and style of risk taking?

I know, I was first talked into a trading style that was not suitable to me. Worst, I had a contract to fulfill and stay beyond my desire to trade that way.

What to look for in a broker

- Honesty - first and foremost
- Service (have desk (floor) access as well as technology)
- Open minded (will not tell you what is good for you and how you should trade)
- Be knowledgeable in all forms of futures even if you get the discount service

Your own criteria may vary. I've brought up some common sense ideas that many novice traders overlook but you are welcome to complement mine.

I hate to be thought of as a number, a file in a 'system'. Personal attention and one-on-one service always gets me. This is how I feel about banks and other institutions.

Deep discount brokers

Commissions are always under scrutiny and pressure when dealing with highly volatile markets such as futures. Many people want no interference and any input from brokers. Typically day traders are such people. This is fine and dandy. There are lots of traders who trade so frequently that for them making money or not will depend on the commissions. There are brokers who will offer access to markets but you are left to fend for yourself and there is no service whatsoever.

Some deep discounters do not even have floor access or the floor desk is backed up and very hard to get through. Bad fills and any disputes with deep discounters is of course a moot point. Often due to bad advice the trader will trade markets that they have no business to and use trading styles that will beg the floor to rip them off. All of the sudden the $2.5 commission RT will be a $75 cost including slippage. Recently I have heard of a $2.5 slippage in gold – that is a $250 "commission"!

I have learned many lessons throughout my 15-year trading career. **The most important is that support positively affects outcome.**
Although trading is an individual pursuit, having a team to support your development and performance as a trader is imperative. Meaningful support, total professionalism and a commitment to deliver the best trading technologies make up the foundation upon which many successful brokerages were built, and through which many traders thrive.

Trading for a Living — Should I Tell the Boss

When asked why they trade people often mumble something evasive about early retirement and how they like the markets. The real truth is many people never ask themselves these uncomfortable questions. Often they subconsciously know the answer and rather not face up to it.

Many traders trade because, let's face it majority of people hate their jobs and even if the do not they feel insecure and unsure of the future and the prospect of the job market as they grow older.

The godsend of a job — no matter how tedious it maybe is the steady income it affords us. Unless you are independently wealthy you will need money to live on and funds to trade. Actually it is a good idea to separate these two if you are planning to trade full time.

While learning and if employed in a decent paying job I cannot emphasize the benefit of not depending on your trading income alone. It is a huge pressure and you do not need it in the top of the already exciting markets and ups and downs.

Certain style of trading is impossible for a part-time trader others are quite possible to trade only taking one hour a day.

People who quit jobs to move into trading are invariably mesmerized with day trading and the prospect of cash flow every day. They take the plunge only to realize that the vast majority of the day-traders lose and even the remainder are often only making minimum wage.

If you have an education and marketable skills you are better off trading part time and earning a salary.

Just like a doctor and a lawyer needs long time to study and equal amount of time to *practice* and hone his/hers skills — a trader needs long practice and theoretical knowledge to come up against the crème de la crème.

A good foundation, practical know-how and amble amount of money can set you on the right track. You too can be part of this phenomenal business that many only dream about.

I would caution anyone after reading this book and trade a few trades part time to just waltz into the Boss office and tell him or her "to take this job and shove it".

Trading as a business is a little more complicated than that. First off - there are many mediocre doctors and lawyers who somehow get by because **they show up in time**. Unfortunately in trading this will not measure up. I strongly caution people to speculate for a longer timeframe because it will allow them to keep that day-job and the paychecks coming.

Of course some people will not listen to me and will enter trading as a full time business. The reason is that there is many business structures that allow traders to speculate in an office environment and will even bestow them the professional title.

Multiple source of income

I do not know who invented this. It has become the buzzword for the Internet and for the myriads of entrepreneurial people who decided that 9-5 lifestyle and corporate politics was not for them. I know that the terminology was some goofy MLM sales pitch but I will take the liberty and use it here.

Trading is a great career for retired military, retired cops anyone who has some money coming to them on a regular basis risk free.

When people ask me why I teach and write instead of trading all the time I tell them the God's honest truth; because I believe this "Multiple source of income" theorem for speculation and trading is crucial to survival and prospering in the pool full of sharks.

Actually I am driven and a good teacher. People like my style of writing and I think I get my point across in a straightforward way.

People who knock others for teaching and offering advice are woefully ignorant of the life as a full time trader.

So you see it is wise to strive for a business related to the markets, in assuring that you will get some mortgage money when you need it.

Speculating with scared money is a curse. Do not do it.

Spread Trading

Spread trading is not a much-heralded hyped up technique this alone should open your eyes to its merits and benefits.

What is spread trading?

Spread trading is buying a commodity contract for one delivery month and selling a different month of the same commodity at the same time.

Spreads are more known for seasonal type speculations and intermediate time trading but spread can surely be applied to Position Trading and long term style trading as well.

There are a number of ways the Speculator can accomplish spread trading:
- Inter-market Spreading
- Intra-market Spreading
- Inter-exchange Spreading
- Owning the physical (underlying commodity) and offsetting with the futures contract (this also called hedging)

Inter-market Spreads

This type of spreading the speculator is buying one commodity (Corn) and selling a different commodity (Soybeans). Inter-market spreads can also be considered Intra-market (calendar) spreads if the speculator buys and sells different delivery month.

Intra-market Spread

This type of a spread is also called a *calendar spread* because the only difference between the buy and sell side of the spread is the delivery month. An example of a Intra-market spread is being long Dec Corn and short July Corn.

The obvious advantage using a spread is the margin requirement.

The margins are set by the exchanges based on the volatility and perceived risk of holding a contract by the customer. Intra-market spreads typically require 25 to 75-precent less of a margin than the outright futures position.

To illustrate the power of spreads lets look back at the silver market in the 1980's inflationary times. As some of you may recall gold and silver had a tremendous bull run in 1980. Holding one contract of silver took $50,000 margin deposit a spread position could be put on for a measly $1500.
Some index futures are still prohibitively expensive for the average investor – using spreads makes speculating in these instruments affordable to almost anyone.

Spreads tend to trend much more dramatically than outright futures contracts. They trend without the interference and noise caused by computerized trading, scalpers, and market movers. Let's look at June Live Cattle
It is often asked how can one predict the spread trend when the chart is not filled with adverse price action and zigzag like the outright

Parabolic SAR

Some people feel uncomfortable about trading spreads since it cannot easily execute **stop loss orders.** Actually stop loss is a hassle that you may not even want to deal with. The parabolic SAR can act as a visual tool and when markets turn for your spread you can just get out with a **MOO (Market on Open** on both legs).

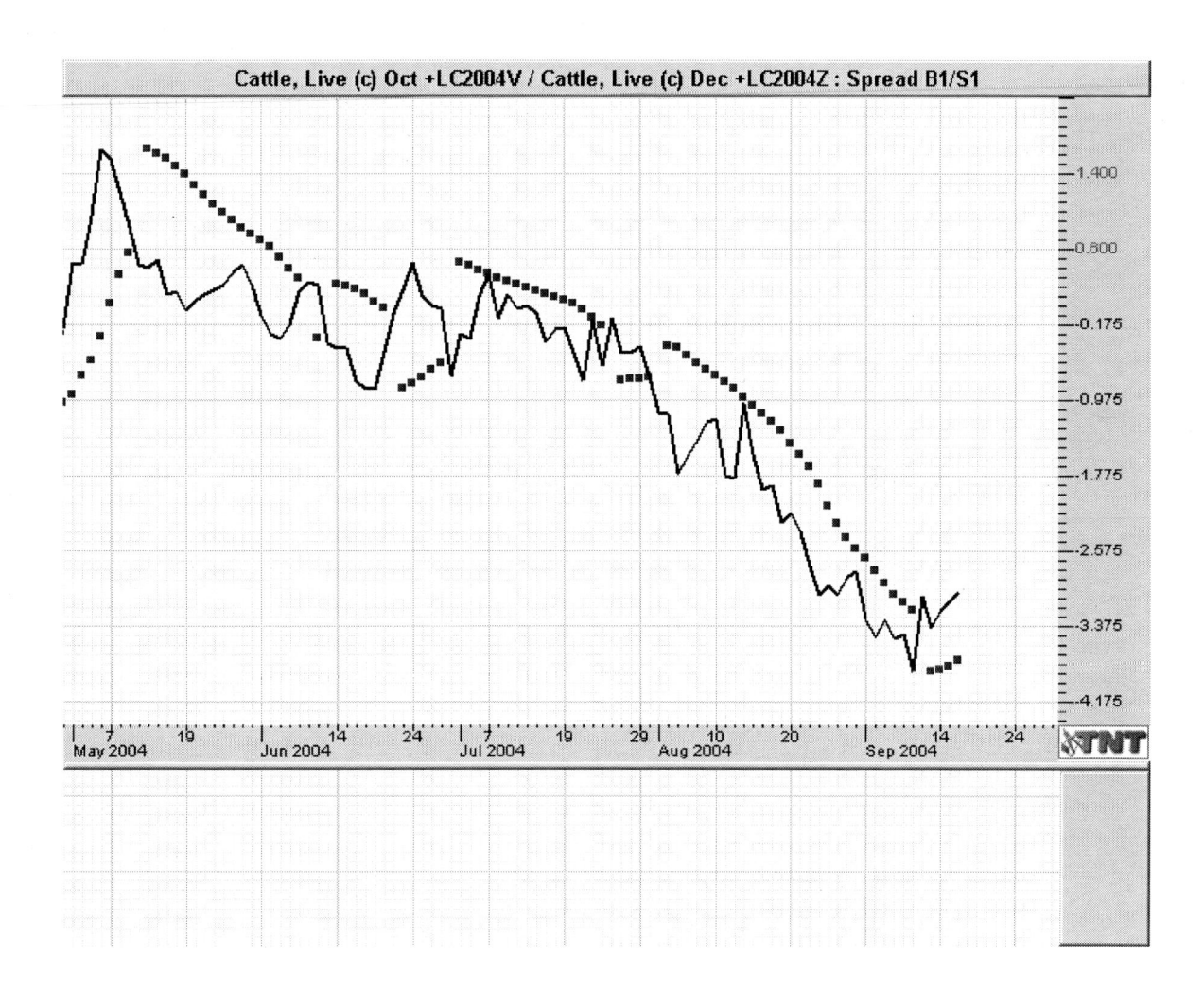

Chart 2

At no time should the reader allude to think that spread trading is risk free only that spreads **usually** carry a much smaller risk as to outright long or short positions. If mini contracts can be traded in lieu of spreads and the underlying risk parameters and financials add up to the prospective speculator he/she may choose trading the mini contracts outright.

(There are some other considerations when selecting to trade minis versus spreads and I will get to these further down in this Chapter)

The additional benefit of trading spreads is the affordable way of getting live experience in futures trading with out risking a fortune and losing sleep and lots of money.

Let us look at some fundamental characteristics of commodity spreads.

Normal markets the current prevailing interest rate has bearing on the price of the future. This typically applies to storable commodities only.

This factor is called a *carrying charge* the following formula can be applied to calculate it;

The current prime rate + 1% are multiplied by the market price of the commodity using the price quoted for the nearest month. Divide the result by 12 and then the monthly storage and insurance cost is added.

The full carrying price is seldom paid in real life. The carrying price is more realized in bearish markets and gets narrowed under bullish conditions.

Let is look at an example:

At the time of the writing of this book July wheat is quoted at $4.14 (414c) a bushel.

Consider prime rate at 1% (414 x .02) / 12 = 0.69 cent.

Storage and insurance is about 4.5 cents per bushel. So the full carrying charge is about 5.0 cents.

Scarcity in the commodity can cause the carrying charge to be *inverted, which* means that the nearby futures are priced at a premium over the deferred, further out futures.

As you see the current time when interest rate is depression level low the interest rate portion of the carrying charge is negligible. However in normal times when rates are higher, the carrying charge is more comprises of the interest rate. Let us look at a more normal 5 percent prime rate:

Lets look at the same Wheat at $4.14 (414c) a bushel and prime rate at 5% (414 x .06) / 12 = 2 cent.

A typical *bullish spread* the speculator would initiate by being long the nearest month and sell a further out month.

A typical *bear market* the speculator would initiate by being short the nearest and buy the more distant month.

Bear spreads must be handled with care since the profit potential of such trades is limited by the carrying changes but their loss potential is unlimited should the trader have gauged the market wrong.

This above synopsis show how most storable commodities behave that can be delivered and by no means can be applied as a general rule.

For example stock indices like the SP 500 behave exactly the opposite and as a bull spread you should sell the nearby and buy the further out month.

Gold and silver market typically behaves inverted in a great calamity where there is huge speculative interest and hoarding. (As we have seen it in the 80's inflationary years)
In those markets when wishing to jump on the bandwagon you should sell the nearby month and go long the further out months as the nearby is at a premium that premium is fluff. This tactic can be a little dangerous as the inverted spread can have an elasticity of a very large rubber band.

Stop loss order should be used especially with bear spreads where the profit potential is limited but the loss is in theory unlimited.

Point Spreads and Money Spreads

A typical *Point Spread* is when a buying and selling is measured in identical units.
A typical inter-delivery spread would be May/July soybeans. If the price difference at the initiation of May minus July is minus 10 cents.

The fact is that the spread is a negative number (-10c) means that the July contract is 10c higher priced than the May contract.

The typical *money spread* involves live cattle versus live hogs. This is a scenario when the contracts are in different contract sizes (a cattle contract is 40,000 lbs and the hog contract is only 30,000 lbs). So when we buy one contract of live hogs 67 cents and sell one contract of a cattle contract at 83 cents we can not only look at the price difference of 16 cents when in reality 1 cent move in cattle is worth $400 and 1 cent in hogs is worth $300.

These examples are not suggestions to trade in light of true Position Trading. Buying hogs is only prudent when we have a tend signal for hogs and selling cattle only would muddy the waters. The position may work out famously or may not. Obviously one could think of this example as a great idea in light of mad cow disease and possible decent exports forecast of hogs to China for example.

The only true limited risk spread is an inter-delivery spread initiated not too far from the factual carrying charges, which are loss-limiting factors.

Good markets to trade using inter-delivery spreads are energy, grains metals.
In metals it is typical to trade gold against silver or platinum against gold. The platinum marker is so thin and tightly controlled by the Russians that trading it by itself could be a problem.

The other good spreading market to trade is currencies.

Let us say for example that we are bearish the dollar. We could simply sell the dollar index and expect a rough ride and some volatility, or we can buy the Swiss franc and sell the Euro. The later position has smaller profit potential but takes less money to initiate and it also takes less antacid and sleepless nights.

Profit potential

When calculating profit potential we should keep in mind the risk taken on via volatility and leverage. The leverage on spreads is inherently lower since one position always offsets the other.

How should you trade spreads?

Selecting a seasoned and professional broker or software can be a great asset. Most brokers and pundits mention spread in a same breath are usually referring option spreads. You must make it clear with the prospective broker firm what you do and check the firm's reputation and credentials carefully.

Both 'legs' of the spreads should be traded at one time. Professionals trade on and off the floor commodity spreads actively. There is seldom any problem getting a quote for a given spread irrespective if the market is open outcry of electronic.

Spread trading is an art and a science. You should immerse and study it well. This chapter is not intended to replace a serious book or familiarization with this subject.
I personally rather buy the futures outright and use stops. If I can't muster the high margin I would use mini contracts or even spread betting shops in England.

There are circumstances however when you get a trend signal and should use spreads. I am talking specifically about currencies. You may not get the same "bang for the buck" but your timing can be a little off and volatility and margins will not hurt you as much either.

Seasonality

Many people trade spreads based purely on seasonal patterns. Seasonal factors sometimes work but sometimes they do not. Remember there are no silver bullets.

I suggest keeping and open mind if you decide to study spread trading. Do not box yourself into a perceived holly grail theory nor should you discard any theories based on my Course.

Spread order specifics

The **buy side** always comes first. Your order must clearly state the quantity and month of the contract. Spell out the numbers. Say, "15 – one five" or "50 – five zero". When you say the contract months, September and December are easy to mix-up. Say instead: Sep or Dec and spell it out. Spell out your name and give the account number to the Clerk.
Always give the spread differential. Never mention the price on the individual contract legs; after all you do not care where the individual was bought as long as **the spread** you got it is adequate to your plans.

Using MOC orders is a good idea for spreads. I will explain why in a moment.

This is what you can also do; you can have an order to exit a spread by doing so Market on Close (MOC) or **leg out** using two separate futures orders Market on Close. It does not make any sense to watch a spread trading **intra-day**. The legs of the spread will not trade equally and so the spread jumps all over the place during the day.

The only thing important about a spread as far as entry and exit are concerned is the Close. Many spreads, if entered during the day will not be desirable by the end of the day. The same thing is true for exiting a spread. Many spread which are exited during the day at a loss end up profitable by the end of the day.

Over the period of a series of trades, entering and exiting based on the Close will prove statistically to be as successful as driving yourself crazy watching them during the day.

Late reporting

Spreads traded for grains on the CBOT floor have issues with late reporting and other annoyances. These markets are not electronic and flash fills are not yet offered. So when you get your spread order reported is anybodies guess.

Seasonality in Spreads

Track 'n Trade has a seasonality plug-in with 10 and 15-year data provided for each commodity contract. This can be very beneficial for those who took it upon themselves to study seasonal patterns in futures trading.

For both the 10-year and 15-year the seasonal probability is much better. Feeder Cattle prices reach their seasonal lows during October-November period. By December prices begin to rise, and tend to rise through February and into the spring.

Chart 3

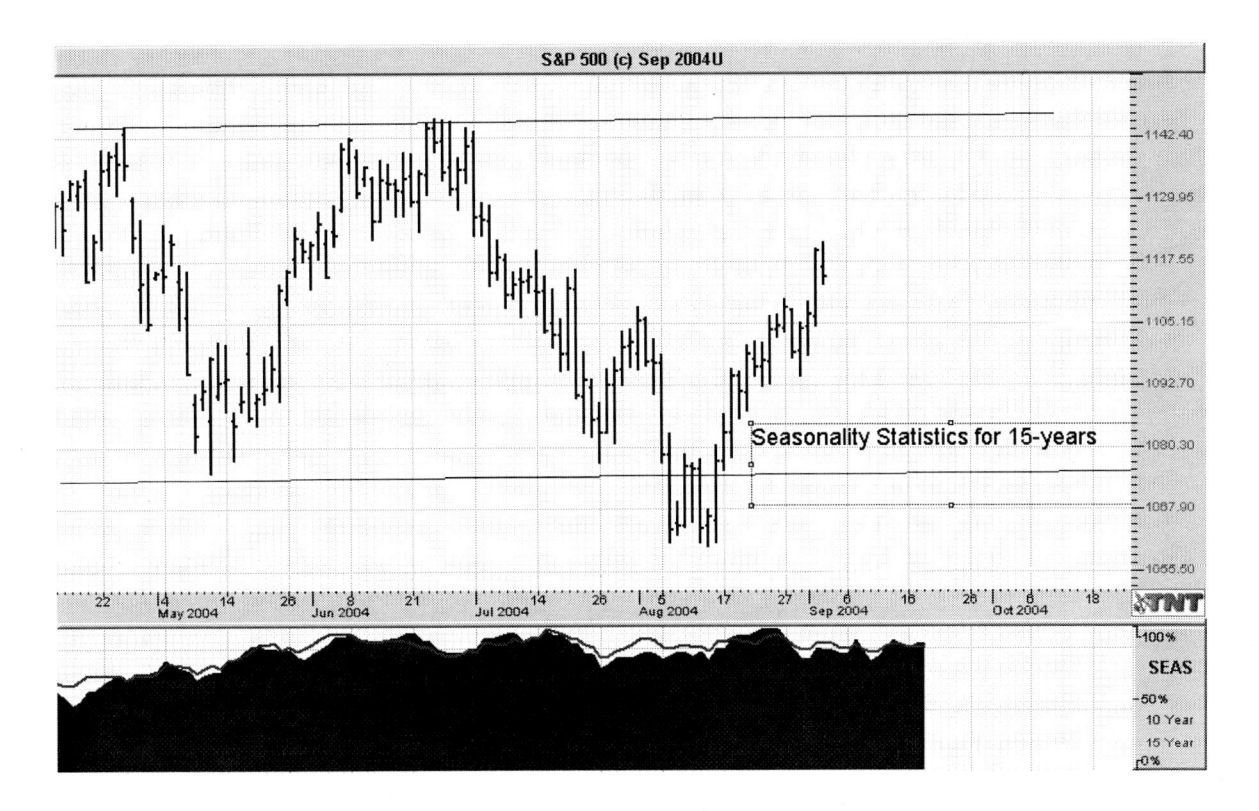

Track 'n Trade's **SEAS** charts show behavior on a relative basis, meaning the actual prices are not forecasted, just the relative position of the market versus its contract high and low. On the seasonal charts, the high is showed as 1.0, or 100%, while the low is showed as 0.0 or 0%. All similar trading days are lined up for X number of years (the default in Track 'n Trade Pro are 10 years for Trend 1, and 15 years for Trend 2) and are analyzed in terms of where each day falls as a percentage of the highest and lowest price of either the last 12 months or the life of the contract for each specific contract. These prices are then averaged and the average is showed in the indicator window. When the trend line is at 100% or 1.0, it indicates where the contract has on average been at its highest value for specified time range and scale period.

Seasonality is usually reflected in spread trading as we buy or sell the carrying charge or the monthly differential between the two months. It is typical to play off old crop against the new crop.

Things to Remember in Seasonal Spreading

Livestock has no **carrying charge** since by definition livestock is not a storable commodity. In metals the carrying charge is largely dependent on the cost of borrowing money i.e. interest rates.

Lumber prices have strong seasonal tendencies; the interest rate factor can enlarge, cancel or reverse the seasonal price moves. This was very prominent in the 1980's when prime rate was double digits and fell to single digits in a few months.

For Energy complex, the month of July marks the peak of U.S. summer driving season. February is the peak of the heating season, however this may wary. In other years, late December maybe the peak for heating season. The energy markets never pay more than full carry, but there is theoretical limit on an inversion. This means that traders can cap their losses when speculating carry-market situations but can really take a hit in non-carry-markets.

The Spreader's Thought Process

Why people do not trade spreads more often? The main reason is the *seemingly* difficult analysis and thought process that involves the market selection, profit analysis and general decision-making process in spread trading. It is however complicated only on the surface. Most traders learn chart patters and set ups looking at price, volume and open interest of one futures contract. Just that exhausts some people.

A spreader must look at the relative strength of each contract months. One trader who perfected his analysis was Richard D. Wyckoff.

Richard D. Wyckoff

In his course, Richard D. Wyckoff stated the basics of his method in five steps:

Step 1: Determine the present position and probable future trend of the market. Then decide how you are going to play it: long, short or neutral.

Step 2: In a bull market, select from those contract months or futures in harmony with the market the ones that are stronger than the market. In a bear market, select those that are weaker than the market.

Step 3: Using point and figure charts, select those futures (or contract months) that have built up a potential count for a move in keeping with your goals.

Step 4: Determine each contract month's readiness to move. Analyze the vertical and figure charts of the candidates with the help of the buying and selling tests.

Step 5: Time your commitments with a turn in the market.
We do not need to use point and figure however this is obviously a technicality and very subjective issue. I do not use point and figure while many people swear by them.

Computers and Technology

This is a very subjective area. Many speculators have no problem spending large sums on redundant computer systems, two broadband Internet connections (one Cable, one DSL). Two monitors and fancy real time quote service. Add some first class news service and you are paying $1000/month before you made a dime trading.
It all depends on your style and business plan.
Generally speaking – more the frequency of your trades better you will need redundancy and real time information (including news). This is at least my experience.
In additions - futures traders are often in need of weather data for drought situations and storm conditions.
The Internet has made life very different for traders and information marketers. Less than 200 years ago we transmitted prices via ticker tapes and cabled buy sell instructions into brokers. Now we can trade in and out of electronic markets with the ease of the locals on the floor.
Having said this - technology can fail. It happens all the time. Orders get stuck, servers go down and Internet slows down due to viruses and other factors. This is the fact of life.
Service becomes important when these things happen. It is nice when you can telephone your broker an order to get you out of the market due to problems with your Internet or local connection. Redundancy is a godsend.

The other factor is the cost. When the United States was in its infancy many people feverishly minded for gold. Some found a lot; some found nothing and many got killed. The people who survived and prospered were those who sold the supplies to the gold miners. You know - shovels, picks and dynamite. It is similar to any business. If the old, gold rush day the savvy marketers had invented the magic gold sniffing dogs and magic "turbo" shovel undoubtedly people would have bought that too. Maybe people had more common sense back then. Nowadays price sums can be spent on the most expensive software, computer hardware and other gadgets. Chat-rooms, member only web sites and other assortments of tools to make you a better trader are available for a price, of course.

It may not be a bad idea to tally up the monthly expense and realize that you will need to make that every month – rain or shine **just to break even**.

Some tools are of course a necessity. Having a computer is not a luxury nowadays. If you shop around carefully you will of course see huge variance in prices depending on whom you are buying from.

Real time of end-of-day quotes

Of course the real time will cost more. Do you need real-time quotes? It will largely depend on the trading style you select and the frequency of trades you need to make.

Cleanliness and delay in "real-time" data

This can be a very annoying problem to day-traders. After spending a pricey sum monthly of real time streaming data you find that real time is actually a 30-seconds delay and there are consistent inaccuracies in the prices reported. This can cost you money and you are paying for the problem.

It is always a good idea to opt for a trial service with amble provisions to cancel and compare the prices and speed of streaming data with a comparable service. Call a trading buddy and compare real time prices. This is the only way I know to keep quote providers honest.

Conclusion

There is not right or wrong in this argument. It is not my task or even my goals to convince you of either use the concepts outlined hereon or totally abandon it. The ultimate decision is with you.

Volume and Open Interest

Volume and open interest will give you an ex-ray picture of what is taking place in the market. I do not like predictive trading but it is elementary to the trader to be able to and strive 'to predict' prices to some extent. Just understand the higher risk and inherent limitation of predictability of *any* market. I do believe that market selection has a great deal to do whether you can benefit and profit from this strategy.

To illustrate lets look at Crude oil chart.

Chart 4

It is my experience that many people either ignore this functionality or have charts that are inadequate in showing open interest and volume data.

The "ten commandments" of volume and open interest are as follows;

When prices are increasing and volume is also increasing this can be interpreted as a bullish sign. What is taking place that shorts are offsetting (or being squeezed?)

Open Interest – terminology

Open interest is contracts that were bought and sold and *have not been offset*. Each open position has two parties for this calculation only one side of the contract is counted.

- When the slope of volume building up. Even after the initial buildup you could have taken a position only to be met a bigger slope and bullish prices.

    Notice the open interest has the gradual slope initially.

- When Prices are decreasing on increasing volume it is a bearish sign. Due to new selling pressure the longs are offsetting.

- Prices increasing on decreasing volume are a bearish sign. Buying pressure is drying up. A change in price direction is likely.

- Prices decreasing on falling volume are a bullish sign. Indicating a possible turn.

- Prices increasing on increasing open interest. A bullish sign. Increasing open interest (OI) indicates NEW buying.

Notice the increase of the slope for **open intcrest** after the turn in the market in late June. Also notice that the **volume** has remained relatively the same during all this.

- Prices decreasing on increasing open interest. A bearish sign - new selling is coming to market

- Prices are increasing on decreasing open interest. A Bearish sign – shorts are offsetting.

It is interesting to notice how open interest first mild slow and then a free falling from the shorts leaving and licking their wounds. It is likely that some traders were expecting a double top first and the market moved up a little and actually forming a strange looking quad top before falling off.

- Prices are decreasing on decreasing open interest. Also a bearish sign. Longs are offsetting.

- Prices are increasing on increasing volume and open interest. This is extremely bullish. This is often a precursor to a much higher price in the future.

- Prices are decreasing on increasing volume and open interest. Very bearish sign. The logic behind it is the reverse as rule 9.

Why Speculators Fail?

It is a good idea to study *failure* to avoid it. I do not like to dwell upon failure as looking and adopting success is a better model sometimes.

This chapter however will focus on losing mindset and actions typically attributed to losing traders.

1. Failure to have a trading plans

A trader with no specific plan of action in place upon entry into a futures trade is like a rudderless ship - ready to run over a coral reef luring beneath the waves.

2. Inadequate trading capital or improper money management

It does not take a fortune to trade futures markets with success. Traders with less than $5,000 in their trading accounts can and do trade futures successfully. And, traders with $50,000 or more in their trading accounts can and do lose it all in a heartbeat if they trade too big relative to the capital.

3. Expectations that are too high, too soon.

Beginning futures traders that expect to quit their "day job" and make good living trading futures in their first few years of trading are usually disappointed. You don't become a successful doctor or lawyer or business owner in the first couple years of the practice. It takes hard work and perseverance to achieve success in any field of endeavor-and trading futures is no different.

4. Failure to use protective stops or at least mental stops.

Using protective buy stops or sell stops upon entering a trade provide a trader with a good idea of about how much money he or she is risking on that particular trade, should it turn out to be a loser. Protective stops are a good money-management tool, but are not perfect (see my section on stops). There are no perfect money-management tools in futures trading.

5. Lack of "discipline."

Don't trade just for the sake of trading or just because you haven't traded for a while. Let those very good trading "set-ups" come to you, and then act upon them in a prudent way. The market will do what the market wants to do-and nobody can force the market's hand.

6. Trading against the trend-or trying to pick tops and bottoms in markets.

It's human nature to want to buy low and sell high (or sell high and buy low for short-side traders). Unfortunately, that's not at all a proven means of making profits in futures trading. Top pickers and bottom-pickers usually are trading against the trend, which is a major mistake.

7. Letting losing positions ride too long.

Most successful traders will not sit on a losing position very long at all. They'll set a tight protective stop, and if it's hit they'll take their losses (usually minimal) and then move on to the next potential trading set up. Traders, who sit on a losing trade, "hoping" that the market will soon turn around in their favor, are usually doomed.

8. "Over-trading."

Trading too many markets at one time is a mistake-especially if you are racking up losses. If trading losses are piling up, it's time to cut back on trading, even though there is the temptation to make more trades to recover the recently lost trading assets. It takes keen focus and concentration to be a successful futures trader. Having too many open trades at one time is a mistake.

9. Failure to accept complete responsibility for your own actions.

When you have a losing trade or are in a losing streak, don't blame your broker or someone else. You are the one who is responsible for your own success or failure in trading. You make the trading decisions. If you feel you are not in firm control of your own trading, then ask yourself why? You should make immediate changes that put you in firm control of your own trading destiny.

10. Not getting a bigger-picture perspective on a market.

One can look at a daily bar chart and get a shorter-term perspective on a market trend. But a look at the longer-term weekly or monthly chart for that same market can reveal a completely different picture. It is prudent to examine longer-term charts, for that larger perspective, when contemplating a trade.

What is the proper mindset of the winning trader?

Well for one – never underestimate the market or think in terms of how much you can make on an individual trade. That is a losing proposition. It will box you into this one particular trade and set you up for failure should something go wrong.

In my opinion - positive thinking is not a prerequisite or even a good trait in trading.

Instead a prudent speculator will ask and prod his mind what can go wrong in each and every position he/she enters BEFORE he committed any money.

Fading over-bough and over-sold markets is not a totally bad idea provided absence of a strong trend. Even in very strong markets there are periods when there is an over-bought condition materialize and it is prudent to sell. In other words even in the strongest markets prices never move up in a straight line.

Smart traders will always keep in mind the mode for the day. Is the mode bullish or bearish? The tone is usually set at the opening and during that time you will gauge the mood for that day. There can be a long-term bullish chart for crude but intermediate trend can be very bearish and couple that with a bearish day you certainly will not profit by going long. So when people tell you next time that aged old fable "the trend is your friend" it is always are nice comeback to ask which trend they are specifically refereeing at.

Let's look at the major long-term trend in crude. Is this a buy here or a sell provided the market fails to follow through?

What would caution us from this trade is the volume has not fallen that much and open interest is also still high - a sign that the down move likely to continue. Other indicators all would tell us to stay pay or get short.

So here is a long-term chart with an intermediate short-term reversal. The intermediate and short-term trend is **bearish**.

Many novices fall into this trap and would buy only to be stopped out or worst lose more to the more experienced and more cautious traders. Remember trading futures is a zero sum game.

Trading is not an exact science and many contradictions would exist to befuddle the novice trader. The difference of the move from the trend-line to where the market eventually turned was around $3200 on one contract. That is no small change.

Market selection

Big mistake traders make is not selecting their markets carefully. Any market you trade needs to be studies and investigated prior risking any money. The description below is only guidance and represents my opinion. Your take may vary. I suggest you read my take and study and investigate these markets before form you opinion. The whole idea of my list is to show that not all markets are created equal and some are better than the others,

1. British Libor - No.

2. British Pound - OK, but choppy. Trade Euro/Yen/Swiss instead

3. Canadian Dollar - Yes

4. Coffee - Yes, but beware of strong limit moves & gaps

5. Copper - OK - better to follow gold/silver though

6. Corn - Good, very small contract size

7. Cotton - Very Good

8. Crude-Oil - Good. Handle with care on API report days

9. Euro - Very good

10. Eurodollar - Very liquid, boring most of the time, but can be a strong "trender"

11. Gold - Historically a little difficult, but probably best contract to have your metals section covered

12. Japanese Yen - very good

13. Live Cattle - OK, a bit seasonal

14. Lumber - Does trend but can do nothing for long periods

15. NYSE Composite Index - I would stay clear of stock indices for commodity trend trading when starting out.

16. Orange Juice - I didn't really get on with the old juice.

17. Palladium. Not liquid.

18. Pork Bellies. The classic. I have had some good moves on it. Fairly liquid but chops sometimes

19. S&P 500 Index. Forget it, as above.

20. Soybean Oil. Good, small contract size. But there is no point trading all 3 of the soybean complexes unless you are spreading.

21. Swiss Franc - Very good

22. T-Bills - Illiquid

23. T-Bonds - Very good

24. T-Notes - Very good

25. Unleaded Gasoline - I would stick to crude oil. However look for leadership from this contract for the kick off of "summer driving season".

26. Wheat - Good. It can be a little choppy.

27. Sugar – Good. It trends very nicely.

This is not a complete list since I put it together many electronic contracts opened up on Globex trading.

Indeed when I look at the Palladium chart we can look up the daily volume and there are some days when the market trades on very light volume. This is a very simple test to gauge a market's viability is to look at the daily volume. If the daily volume is not in several thousands you may not want to trade that stock or commodity.

My 'super special' secrets

Your initial entry in trading should be accompanied with a goal – that goal is to survive. You cannot enter into trading part time or full time and have unreasonable expectations. Your first goal is to try to beat your bank rate or savings. Let's say you're getting 2-percent, set a modest goal of 6-8-percent return.

The best money managers do not have 50-60 percent returns so you can't expect yourself outperform them.

You will achieve success by **not** trading a lot. You will not take chances and do a lot of your training on paper and learning about charting.

You will **not** trade full sized leveraged instruments.

Finding your own way and technique is very important. You can't tell someone to do this and that when that person is not ready or comfortable doing so.

The system you use

- Must fit your pocketbook and fiscal situation
- Must also match your psychological makeup and personality
- Must fit the time allowed to trade – full-time trader versus part-time trader

Earlier I have alluded to the fact that there are "times" and "surfer" in trading. If your core belief system is such that anyone can master and learn proper timing and gain positive expectation then no amount of lecturing and course writing will help to disperse that.
On the other hand if you find that timing is elusive and hard to learn than you can trade like many – go with the flow.
The best way to find your way is to use a good simulator. This brings us back to the tools you use. Check out a few and make comparisons. There should be no reason that you must use one over the other. See what makes you at ease.

When you find a system that fits you, trade it on the **Track "N Trade Pro** simulator along side your "real money" platform. Trade on the **Track "N Trade Pro** and take notes what happens to your trades before and after.

Learn the high probability set-ups. Using Track "N Trade Pro it is very easy!
Now this might entail trading the simulator for most of the day, but
You will learn by *repetition* and discover when you get near the high probability set-up
NOW YOU CAN SWITCH ON THAT ONE TRADE TO REAL!

Do you see it? Your busy trading all day but you have only placed one real trade a day…As you progress you can use this method on other systems and maybe 2 or 3 trades for real. But it is important to read the market with your simulator first **then move to real money trading.**

This method works for some people and for others it is not appropriate. All I can say is trying won't hurt. Oh, by the way my secret is – **"there are NO SECRETS"**

Foreign Exchange Speculating

Many people do not understand what distinguishes professional speculators from individual efforts to trade. Most experts agree that the key is market selection and uncorrelated portfolio management. In addition of spreading your risk and bets around adding to winners properly is also a lost art and misunderstood by 90-percent of individual traders.

We try to break the barrier with this product and also try to educate individual traders the often their limitation is not only in monetary terms but with proper methodology and mindset.

Free Currency Trading Risk and Money Manager

Turbo Turtle™, our proprietary risk management for FOREX market is based on a Percentage Volatility Model (PVM), is a variant of a standard deviation mathematical model.

If nothing else it can serve a purpose to hands on illustrate portfolio management and proper way of looking at risk management in a way Hedge funds do. This is the reason the author offers this software for free to anyone who might benefit from it.

Volatility as a central dispersion measurement of the mean is used in many mathematical models and it is crucial to analyze the dispersion on any time series.

For our purpose a very important factor to take it into account when trading is to place adequate stop orders and finding appropriate entry and exit levels. Since supply and demand drives markets in general, it is our commitment to discover the true volatility of the market once a trend has been defined. Turbo Turtle ™ utilizes algorithms to assess that volatility. By doing this, certain trades are either denied or accepted based on a percentage in relationship to risk/reward parameters that are set in advance.

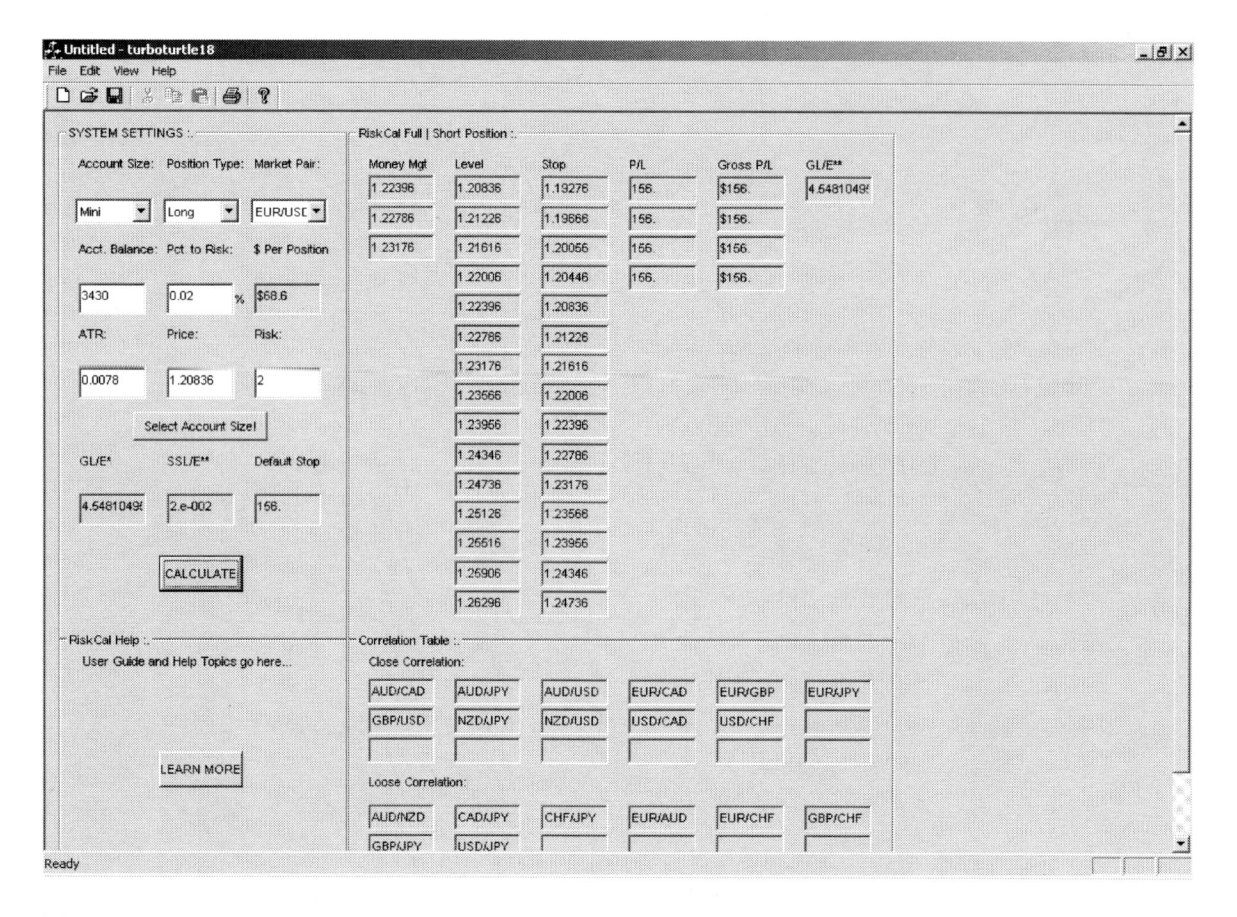

Figure 9

Account Size – select either full ($100,000 lot) or ($10,000 mini lot)

Position Type – long or short

Account Balance – must be the figure from the FX trading account for the current day.

Price – type in the FX rate bought or sold prior (the price your system or signal will provide)

The Percent risk on the position will come up after the calculation; risks over 2.19 are not advisable to take. Notice this figure changes depending on your Account Balance and ATR levels (see explanation below).

Stop

The right hand side of the software panel will show you the stop levels. While it is calculated to 10-levels we typically only use the first three. Moves in FX are large but seldom warrant 10-levels of pyramiding.

Money Management

This is the price target for the position. The third level, it is optional if you use it or not.

Level

This column is the price of entry i.e. the rate the currency pairs were bought or sold.

The other side of the panel has three levels of Price Targets and Stops pre-calculated. The Target prices can be entered in your Execution software[4] at the first purchase time.

Notice - We recommend profit targets on the first two positions and no target on the last one. The profit targets will limit your overall return but also lessen the drawdown for this system. Use or don't use this feature depending on your temperament and financial situation.

We do not tell you what FX broker to use. Nor we religiously tell you the buy and sell signals. We have a trend research facility and systems in place for our coaching clients. We can also make this available to you and/or help you devising a system on which you would base your buy and sell recommendation.

---

[4] This is the software your FX broker provides you

There are two kinds of brokers you can trade currencies with;

Some of them still make the market and trade against you i.e. take the other side of your trade. Having more capital and the information of order flow they have a distinct advantage against you. It is my suggestion to avoid them.

The other kind of a foreign exchange broker is using the ECN model. Orders of various clients are matched in a central computer and trade is made electronically. Here are some ideas:

Transparent Quoting

The most obvious difference between ECN based brokers and the Dealer model is the quoting of Bids and Asks. In the Dealer model it is the dealer who is the only Market Maker and so has the monopoly to offer the trader quotes that are in line or out of line with the real market. This opens the door to questionable practices, because of the fact that the dealer knows all positions and all Orders of each of his clients and can (and likely will) manipulate trading to his own benefit.

The ECN-like-market is very different in this aspect. First, the Broker (*Interactive Brokers* (IB) in this case) does not participate in the trading but instead he facilitates a trading-platform where Market Makers (the big banks) and individual traders can enter their offers. The Market Makers provide most liquidity. They offer quotes and will compete for the orders of the Trader. The Market Makers are not allowed to trade against each other, but the Traders on the other hand have all freedom: they are allowed to trade against each other or take the Market Makers offers.

Obviously, this model has many advantages for the retail-trader. It is transparent and fair as every participant has the same information. Every one can see the Limit-orders and Market Depth book, and no one can see the Stop and Stop Limit orders. Furthermore, because of the fact that many participants can quote, the spread between Bid and Ask will be very tight (half pip is possible).

Fees structure

Although the FX-dealers advertise their business as commission-free, this is far from the real truth. The FX-dealer has to make a living and he does so by quoting the Bid and Ask in such a way that he always gets (at least) 1 pip of every trade.

The ECN-like-broker, on the other hand, charges a fee per Order executed on his trading-platform. The fees calculated by IB are quite competitive. Depending on the Order size it is about 0.5 pip for a 100,000-dollar round-turn trade. You can compare the IB costs with an FX-dealer by adding this 0.5 pip to the bid/ask spread for the particular currency on the ECN. The spread for EUR.USD is 0.5 to 1.5 so including fees it will be 1.0 to 2.0.

But we have to say that the IB-fee is larger when trading the smallest lot of 25.000 dollars. In that case the IB-fee can be 1 pip more, which makes very short-term trading not attractive for very small traders (likewise FX-dealers).

Trading restrictions

Most FX-dealers have certain trading restrictions in place. This is mainly because of the price-monopoly the FX-dealer has, but moreover due to the "relationship" between the Dealer and his Bank. The FX-dealer needs to cover his risk by taking posit positions with his Bank (which has access to the Inter-bank systems). In order to manage his risk he enforces restrictions to his clients. A well-known restriction is that the trader is not allowed to modify his Order when it is 10 pips or less from the current market.
Another restriction, sometimes used, is that the Trader is not allowed to place new trades during volatile times (like big news events).

The ECN-like-broker has no trading restrictions at all.

Account protection

No government control like the CFTC exists for FX-dealers, and no protection by law is in place when the FX-dealer goes bankrupt.

That might be the case with some ECN-like-Brokers as well, but not for IB clients. With IB the account-budget of a Universal-account is registered in the Futures-account, and falls thereby under the CFTC rules. SIPC and Lloyd's of London insure customer funds at IB, denominated in any currency.

Some FX-dealer-like-brokers use sophisticated charting packages some use Java applets only and hence will be very limited in the area or studies and charting.

How to use the Turbo Turtle FX Money/Risk manager?

We do not think money management is the Holy Grail and without an edge your trading will suffer in terms of negative returns, s or infrequent trades. However the best system using no money and position management will also suffer and a good system can become a loser if you take on too much risk relative to your account and/or pyramid incorrectly.

The first three lines on the left side of the panel are of importance. The first and second "Price Target" (Money Management) boxes are to be filled in as limit orders upon getting the first signal. We suggest using price targets on the first two levels.

The *levels* are add on trades and they can also be entered into most FX-dealer's platforms as contingent orders (this is our way of pyramiding when the order is working out)

Notice that some trades are not to be taken and this will depend on the currencies rate and risk per your current account size. If the trade signal has a risk level of larger than 2.19 you should be well advised to avoid that trade and look for a next one. This box is on the left side of the panel under the name "Percent/Risk".

The ATR (Average True Range) for the day is available from most FX-dealer's platforms please consult your platform's recommendation on how to get the ATR level. You can also ask us about the platform we suggest and if you are a consulting client with Turbo Turtle.

The GL/E is the *'gatekeeper'* so you will not trade over the ~2 percent risk. This field depends on the account size.

Important tip

Adjusting the percentage risked is the key to success. In times of high volatility this percentage should be raised and in times of low volatility it should be lowered. Volatility should be distinct to currency pairs. This software however will only take the input you have already determined.

If volatility reaches a certain point cease trading. It is recommended that if ATR doubles from one day to next the market is not tradable as whipsaw potential is more than normal.

Non-correlated positions in a portfolio

Many novice traders and even *experts* do not realize the portfolio correlation issue; of course many do not have adequate funds to even think about a portfolio. The godsend of FX-trading is the flexibility of position size and automatic unit calculation (pip).
This enables the small trader to effectively trade like a hedge fund and hence create an advantage for his/hers trading strategy.

As a reader you can e-mail us with any questions and problems. We want to teach you and help.

The system's power stems from the fact that currencies do trend and if caught a decent move you will make money. You can take small 2 percent losses if you pyramid to three levels and your last position has no pre-calculated target.
The other important issue is spreading your risk wisely. Our correlation tables are proprietary and time tested. This alone is worth the price of the software.

Trading tips for Currency trading

In order to become a successful trader, you must have sufficient risk capital- the loss of some or all of which will neither completely ruin your morale nor adversely affect your lifestyle in any way. In the event of loss, you must be able to handle such an ordeal calmly.

Your mind should be on the market, not on your finances. In order to make the proper trading decisions, you must remain calm and concentrate on the task of trading. You should never use the last remains of your finances for trading- the responsibility and the pressure would be too great, and your mind would stray towards your finances, and not towards the market situation, thus greatly increasing the possibility of mistakes.

Don't rush to open a real account after only a few days of practice. Practice for as much time as is necessary for you to feel confident on your own. Don't compare yourself to other traders- just because it took someone a certain amount of time to become proficient, doesn't mean you won't need more time. Your primary goal when practicing is to develop an individual trading style or technique such that, at the very least, your next week's trade earnings are not less than the current week's, and that your monthly earnings should increase with each successive month. Only after achieving these results, should you open a real account.

Always follow that universal and venerable rule of the market: Cut your losses as soon as possible, and hold your winning positions open as long as possible. Furthermore, do not, under any circumstances, allow loss to occur in a position that has been making profit. It is better to close it altogether without profit if the market suddenly turns in the opposite direction, rather than to allow a profit to turn into loss. That would not be smart.

New traders are not recommended to trade on Sunday nights, New York EST time, because this is actually Monday morning for Asian markets, and the behavior of currencies at this time is the least predictable. It is also not recommended to trade on Fridays, especially in the morning (EST). On Friday the market usually breaks away from the trend that it set during the week, and for the novice, this may come as an unpleasant surprise. Also, on Friday, more often than not, the market has a tendency to sell off American dollars, especially when the US economy is in an uncertain situation.

Try to begin trading at the same time each day. The behavior of currencies differs at different times of the day, and by concentrating on a certain time each day, you may come to understand the characteristic behaviors of currencies at this time. Begin your day by researching events that occurred on the market while you were away from trading. For this purpose, our site has a great feature that will help: "Market News". After familiarizing yourself with the market events, look at the graphs to study the movement of the currencies, starting with "tick" charts and ending with daily charts, and select a tactic that you will use for this particular day.

As rewarding as self-study may be, a more thorough and proper understanding of the market might be achieved through a formal education such as the one that our One on One Coaching provides, in both classroom and correspondence formats. In any case, we recommend that you trade on your demo account daily, and research charts. Profit comes to those who try! Learning to trade on this market is not as difficult as learning the stock market, but it is a gradual process. Only patience and a systematic approach will bring you positive financial results!

Mistakes and losses are an unavoidable part of trading in any market. The sooner you learn to accept losses as inevitable, the sooner you will begin to earn. You should not blame yourself, others, or the market for your losses. Your losses are in no way related to your reasoning abilities. Your task is to calmly analyze your mistakes and to not repeat them in future trades. You should not jump for joy after winning $800, nor beat your head against the wall after losing $200. The less emotions form a part of your trading, your ability to see the true market situation and to make the right decision will improve. It is vital to develop a cold-hearted lack of emotion, and to treat winnings and losses as just numbers- not money. Understand that traders don't learn from their winnings- they learn from their losses. When every loss is perceived as one step towards your next winning trade- you are on the right track.

Keep a diary in which you describe the conditions that led you to make the trading decisions that you did. Write about the market events that influenced your decision to open or close a position. After every trade, write down and analyze the results in your diary. If you made a profit, it is important that you understand and remember your flow of thinking, which led you to the right decision. Market events happen often and new news may replace old news, so you will eventually forget what happened unless you keep track of it yourself. It is even more important to understand why you lost. There are really not that many mistakes that amateur traders commit, and if you can understand them all, you can learn not to repeat them.

Read the opinions of others, but base your trading decisions on your own analysis of, and feel for the market, which you will eventually acquire. If your prediction matches someone else's – all is good. If not, that's not a problem either. However, if upon seeing a disparity, you start doubting your analysis, it would be best not to make the trade on your real account- only on the demo. If you are confident in your decision, go ahead and do it- one of the predictions will be correct. If your prediction is not the correct one, find the fault in your analysis

Remember that if your account contains less than $3000, you should not trade using more than one lot. If you are in the $3000-$5000 range, never trade more than two lots and that if and only if it looks safe in the current market situation. If you have $10,000 in your account you may trade two lots, but never more than three. If you follow these rules, you will considerably limit the risk factor. Trading too many lots at once is dangerous and unwise.

Andras Nagy
http://www.spread-traders.com/

Other Useful Books to Read

There are lot of good books on Investing and Speculating and there is a lot of garbage out there. This list is not complete only represents the *crème de la crème* according to the author.

Reminiscences of a Stock Operator
   By Edwin LeFevre – Published in May 1994

This book is a classic. Not much about Investing and risk management but the psychology of Speculating and making and losing millions. This book is a fictionalized life story of the legendary trader Jesse Livermore.

How I made 2 Million Dollars in the Stock Market
   By Nicholas Darvas

Nicholas Darvas, a Hungarian Born dancer made 2 million dollars in the stock market. Lots of experts in trading and finance agree that his book is the best book written on the stock market and stock investing.

Portfolio Theory and Capital Markets

   By William F Sharpe

This is the bible of Modern Portfolio Theory. William Sharpe's Capital Asset Pricing Model (CAPM) became a linchpin of modern investment theory

Hot Commodities

   By Jim Rodgers

According to Jim Rogers the ex-partner of George Soros the new bull market in America will be in hard assets, commodities and essentials not in Stocks. You could have guessed by now, I agree with Jim.

How I Trade for Living

By Gary Smith

Gary, by his own admission was a vendor when he was promoting his first book
Live the Dream by Profitably Day Trading Stock Futures.
Gary Smith now trades full time and has no outside interests from trading. After many years of breaking even and struggling he finally found his true market. Leveraged Fund trading and market timing. He would not call himself a market timer because he actually day traded Rydex type Mutual Funds. His trading style is very low-key and low tech., plus it works.

Glossary

Arbitrage

What is simultaneous purchasing and selling of identical or equivalent financial instruments or commodity futures in order to benefit from a discrepancy in their price relationship is.

Ask

Also called "offer". Indicates a willingness to sell a futures contract at a given price. (See bid.)

Back Months
The futures or options on futures months being traded that are furthest from expiration.

Bear
One who believes prices will move lower.

Bear Market
A market in which prices are declining.

Bid
The price that the market participants are willing to pay. See offer.

Bull
One who expects prices to rise.

Bull Market
A market in which prices are rising.

Buy On Close
To buy at the end of a trading session at a price within the closing range.

Buy On Opening
To buy at the beginning of a trading session at a price within the opening range.

Cabinet Trade or cab
A trade that allows options traders to liquidate deep out-of-the-money options by trading the option at a price equal to one-half tick.

Call
An option to buy a commodity; security or futures contract at a specified price anytime between now and the expiration date of the option contract.

Cash Commodity

The actual physical commodity as distinguished from a futures commodity.

Close
The period at the end of the trading session. Sometimes used to refer to the closing range. (See opening, the.)

Closing Range (or Range)
The high and low prices, or bids and offers, recorded during the period designated as the official close. (See settlement price.)

Commission (or Round Turn)
The one-time fee charged by a broker to a customer when a futures or options on futures position is liquidated either by offset or delivery.

CFTC
The Commodity Futures Trading Commission as created by the Commodity Futures Trading Commission Act of 1974. This government agency currently regulates the nation's commodity futures industry.

Contract
Unit of trading for a financial or commodity future. Also, actual bilateral agreement between the parties (buyer and seller) of a futures or options on futures transaction as defined by an exchange.

Contract Month
The month in which futures contracts may be satisfied by making or accepting delivery. (See delivery month.)

Day Order
An order that is placed for execution during only one trading session. If the order cannot be executed that day, it is automatically cancelled.

Day Trading
Refers to establishing and liquidating the same position or positions within one day's trading, thus ending the day with no established position in the market.

Deferred
another term for "back months."

Delivery
The tender and receipt of an actual commodity or financial instrument, or cash in settlement of a futures contract.

Exercise Or Strike Price
The price at which the holder (buyer) may purchase or sell the underlying futures contract upon the exercise of an option.

Expiration Date

The last day that an option may be exercised into the underlying futures contract. Also, it is the last day of trading for a futures contract.

Floor Broker
An exchange member who is paid a fee for executing orders for Clearing Members or their customers. A Floor Broker executing orders must be licensed by the CFTC.

Floor Trader
An exchange member who generally trades only for his/her own account or for an account controlled by him/her. Also referred to as a "local."

Futures
A term used to designate all contracts covering the purchase and sale of financial instruments or physical commodities for future delivery on a commodity futures exchange.

Futures Commission Merchant
A firm or person engaged in soliciting or accepting and handling orders for the purchase or sale of futures contracts, subject to the rules of a futures exchange and, who, in connection with solicitation or acceptance of orders, accepts any money or securities to margin any resulting trades or contracts. The FCM must be licensed by the CFTC.

Hedger or Commercial
Commercial or business entity seeking to lay off risk and normalize price fluctuation by counter trading to the actual commodity holding to avoid a loss

Hedge
The purchase or sale of a futures contract as a temporary substitute for a cash market transaction to be made at a later date. Usually it involves opposite positions in the cash market and futures market at the same time. (See long hedge, short hedge.)

Holder
One who purchases an option.

Initial Performance Bond
The funds required when a futures position (or a short options on futures position) is opened. (Previously referred to as Initial Margin)

Limit Order
An order given to a broker by a customer that specifies a price; the order can be executed only if the market reaches or betters that price.

Limit Price
(See maximum price fluctuation.)

Liquidation
Any transaction that offsets or closes out a long or short futures position.

Locked Limit
Daily limit of the commodity price has been reached and trading is suspended until new sellers/or buyers appear. If no new price action surfaces trading for the day is called 'locked limit'

Long
Is who has bought a futures or options on futures contract to establish a market position through an offsetting sale; the opposite of short.

Long Hedge
The purchase of a futures contract in anticipation of an actual purchase in the cash market. Used by processors or exporters as protection against and advance in the cash price. (See hedge, short hedge.)

Margin
(See Performance Bond)

Maintenance Performance Bond (Previously referred as Maintenance Margin)
A sum, usually smaller than--but part of--the initial performance bond, which must be maintained on deposit in the customer's account at all times. If a customer's equity in any futures position drops to, or under, the maintenance performance bond level, a "performance bond call" is issued for the amount of money required to restore the customer's equity in the account to the initial margin level.

Mark-To-Market
the daily adjustment of margin accounts to reflect profits and losses.

Market Order
An order for immediate execution given to a broker to buy or sell at the best obtainable price.

Maximum Price Fluctuation
The maximum amount the contract price can change, up or down, during one trading session, as stipulated by Exchange rules.

Minimum Price Fluctuation
Smallest increment of price movement possible in trading a given contract, often referred to as a "tick."

M.I.T.
Market-If-Touched. A price order that automatically becomes a market order if the price is reached.

Nearby
Nearby is the nearest active trading month of a futures or options on futures contract. Also referred to as "front-month."

Offer
Also called "ask". Indicates a willingness to sell a futures contract at a given price. (See bid.)

Offset
Selling if one has bought, or buying if one has sold, a futures or options on futures contract.

Open Interest
Total number of futures or options on futures contracts that have not yet been offset or fulfilled by delivery. OI is an indicator of the depth or liquidity of a market (the ability to buy or sell at or near a given price) and of the use of a market for risk- and/or asset-management.

Open Order
An order to a broker that is good until it is canceled or executed.

Opening, The
The period at the beginning of the trading session during which all transactions are considered made or first transactions were completed.

Opening Price (Or Range)
The range of prices at which the first bids and offers were made or first transactions were completed.

Option
A contract giving the holder the right, but not the obligation, hence, "option," to buy (call option) or sell (put option) a futures contract in a given commodity at a specified price at any time between now and the expiration of the option contract.

Out-Trades
a situation (typically on the floor) that results when there is some confusion or error on a trade consummated. A difference in pricing, with both traders thinking they were buying, for example, is a reason why out-trade may occur.

Position
An interest in the market, either long or short, in the form of open contracts. (See open interest.)

Performance Bond (Previously referred to as Margin)
Funds that must be deposited as a performance bond by a customer with his or her broker, by a broker with a clearing member, or by a clearing member, with the Clearing House. The performance bond helps to ensure the financial integrity of brokers, clearing members and the Exchange as a whole.

Performance Bond Call
(Previously referred to as Margin Call). It is demand for additional funds because of adverse price movement.

Pit

Location on the floor where the individual commodity contracts are traded i.e. Corn Pit, Soybean pit

Premium
The excess of one futures contract price over that of another, or over the cash market price. The amount agreed upon between the purchaser and seller for the purchase or sale of a futures option -- purchasers pay the premium and sellers (writers) receive the premium.

Put
An option to sell a commodity, security, or futures contract at a specified price at any time between now and the expiration of the option contract.

Rally
An upward movement of prices following a decline; the opposite of a reaction.

Range
The high and low prices or high and low bids and offers, recorded during a specified time.

Reaction
A decline in prices following an advance. The opposite of a rally

Registered Representative
a person employed by, and soliciting business for, a commission house or Futures Commission Merchant.

Round-Turn
Procedure by which a long or short position is offset by an opposite transaction or by accepting or making delivery of the actual financial instrument or physical commodity is a round turn.

Scalp
To trade for small gains. Scalping normally involves establishing and liquidating a position quickly, usually within the same day, hour or even just a few minutes.

Settlement Price
A figure determined by the closing range that is used to calculate gains and losses in futures market accounts. Settlement prices are used to determine gains, losses, margin calls, and invoice prices for deliveries. (See closing range.)

Short
Is who has sold a futures contract to establish a market position and who has not yet closed out this position through an offsetting purchase; the opposite of long.

Short Hedge
The sale of a futures contract in anticipation of a later cash market sale. Used to eliminate or lessen the possible decline in value of ownership of an approximately equal amount of the cash financial instrument or physical commodity. (See hedge, long hedge.)

Size
Number of contracts traded, position size.

Slippage
Occurs when there is a bad fill in open outcry markets. Resting orders can become market orders and if there is a "fast market" condition *slippage* occurs

Speculator
One who attempts to anticipate price changes and, through buying and selling futures contracts, aims to make profits; does not use the futures market in connection with the production, processing, marketing or handling of a product. The speculator *usually* has no interest in making or taking delivery.

Spread
The simultaneous purchase and sale of futures contracts for the same commodity or instrument for delivery in different months, or in different but related markets. A spreader is not so much concerned with the direction in which the market moves, but only with the difference between the prices of each contract.

Stop Order (Or Stop)
An order to buy or sell at the market when and if a specified price is reached.

Tick
Refers to a change in price, either up or down. (See minimum price fluctuation.)

Trend
The general direction of the market.

Volume
Is the number of transactions in a futures or options on futures contract made during a specified period of time.

Writer
An individual who sells (writes) an option.

Index

A
Accumulation/Distribution, 163
Average True Range, 100, 104, 217

B
Bar, 146
Berkshire Hathaway, 179
Beta, 14, 15
Bollinger Band, 159

C
Capital Asset Pricing Model, 222
Charles Faulkner, 169
CIA, 166
CNN, 166
Correlation, 14, 43, 138

D
Daily Price Limits, 147
Dan Akroyd, 170
Directional Movement Indicator, 161
Dr. Brett Steenbarger, 171

E
Edwin LeFevre, 222

F
Fort Knox, 177
Fund Switching, 55

G
Gary Smith, 223
Gecko Software, 165
Geographic Rotation, 55
George Soros, 142, 223
gold standard, 175

H
Hedging, 16, 22

I
Inter-market Spreads, 188
Intra-market Spread, 188

J
James Turk, 178
Jesse Livermore, vii, 77, 222
Jim Rogers, 142, 223
John Sununu, 178

K
Kelly Criterion, 55, 56
kiodiophobic, 12. *See*
kiodiotropic, 12

L
Late reporting, 195
limit-down, 147
limit-up, 147

M
Market on Close (MOC), 195
Market-if-touched orders (MIT), 151
MOC – Market on Close, 152
Momentum (MOM), 157
money spread, 192
MOO - Market on Open, 152
Moving Average Convergence-
    Divergence (MACD), 158
Moving Averages, 156

N
Neuro-Linguistic Programming, 169
Nicholas Darvas, 222

O

Over-trading, 205

P

Parabolic SAR, 159, 189
Percentage Volatility Model (PVM), 10, 212
Pivot Points, 148
Point Spread, 192
Position Limits, 133, 148

R

Rate of Change (ROC), 157
Relative Strength Index, 161
Return/Risk Ratio, 14, 15
Richard D. Wyckoff, 197
Richard Nixon, 175
Roth IRA, 174
Rydex, 223

S

Sector Rotation, 54
Sharp Ratio, 15
Slippage, 147, 230
Smithsonian Agreement, 176

Stochastic, 159
Style Rotation, 54

T

The spread, 146
Tick, 145
Tom Wheat, 175
Track 'n Trade Pro, 196

U

USDA, 167

V

VAR (Value At Risk), 16
Volatility, v, 10, 14, 15, 23, 26, 37, 117, 120, 121, 139, 162, 212, 218
Volume, 162

W

Warren Buffett, 178
William F Sharpe, 222
Williams %R, 159